Touching the Church in Eternity

A Journey Through The Book Of Ephesians

Dr. Lee Ann B. Marino, Ph.D., D.Min., D.D.

Foreword by Anthony Sluzas

Touching the Church in Eternity

A JOURNEY THROUGH THE BOOK OF EPHESIANS

Dr. Lee Ann B. Marino, Ph.D., D.Min., D.D.

- Foreword by Anthony Sluzas -

Published by:
Righteous Pen Publications
(The righteousness of God shall guide my pen)
www.righteouspenpublications.com

All rights reserved. No part of this book may be reproduced or transmitted in any form or by any means, electronic or mechanical, or information storage and retrieval system without written permission from the author.

Unless otherwise noted, Scriptures taken from the **Holy Bible, New International Version ®, NIV® (1984),** Copyright © 1973, 1978, 1984, 2011 by Biblica, Inc.™ Used by permission of Zondervan. All rights reserved worldwide.

All passages marked EXB are from **The Expanded Bible.** Copyright © 2011 by Thomas Nelson. Used by permission. All rights reserved.

All passages marked GW ***are a copyrighted work of God's Word to the Nations.*** Quotations are used by permission. Copyright 1995 by God's Word to the Nations. All rights reserved.

Book classification: Books > Religion & Spirituality > Christian Boks & Bibles > Bible Study & Reference > Commentaries > New Testament > Paul's Letters

Cover photo by Nathan Mullet and interior photo by DNK, both from unsplash.com, are in the Public Domain.

Copyright © 2016, 2025 by Dr. Lee Ann B. Marino.

ISBN: 1-940197-36-8
13-Digit: 978-1-940197-36-4

Printed in the United States of America.

Crucified, raised up from the dead
Led captivity captive, it is finished
Oh, He gave us the keys, His authority
Now we are joint heirs
to the praise of His glory, glory

Upon this rock, You build Your church
And the gates of hell will not prevail (no, no)
When we bind and loose, we proclaim Your truth
And in Jesus' Name, we will not fail
We'll never fail, no

Build Your church
Build Your church
Build it from the ground up
It's Your church
Build Your church
Build Your church
Build it from the ground up
We're Your church

(Maverick City Music, *Build Your Church*)[1]

Table of Contents

Foreword

Touching the Church in Eternity: A Journey through the Book of Ephesians by Apostle Dr. Lee Ann B. Marino is both a deeply scholarly work and a practical handbook on Paul's epistle to the Ephesians. Dr. Marino skillfully takes what is spiritually deep and wide, and makes it not only understandable, but also applicable to our daily lives in the twenty-first century. I believe you will be truly blessed while you study the pages of this book as this epistle to the Ephesians and the exceeding riches of God's grace is thoroughly explained and as the Holy Spirit quickens it in your own heart.

The Apostle Paul addresses his epistle to the Ephesians to a group of believers who are rich beyond measure in Christ, but who continue to live as beggars. Why are they spiritually impoverished? It's because they remain ignorant of the exceeding riches of God's grace, their true wealth in Jesus Christ. No Christian must live in ignorance or as a spiritual beggar when God offers true riches beyond all imagining. To move from poverty to prosperity, believers must first listen and then meditate on what the Word of God says about their true standing and then access it and begin living it by faith. There is no other way.

Apostle Dr. Lee Ann B. Marino is a brilliant Bible teacher and my friend, and you are blessed to be able to embark with her on a wonderful journey deep into Ephesians, and it will be well worth the trip. The Holy Spirit has led her throughout the process of writing this work, and you, the reader, will be greatly enriched because of it. So, open your heart and prepare yourself to receive the Good News of your amazing inheritance in

Christ. You are richer than you realize.

Dear one, get ready to enter your wealthy place and in so doing, you will become equipped to proclaim and explain this Good News and make a powerful difference in this world for Christ!

"Maranatha!"

Evangelist/Teacher Anthony Sluzas

Your Place of Grace Conferences with Anthony Sluzas
www.yourplaceofgrace.com

Morgantown, West Virginia
December 30, 2015

Preface

The Book of Ephesians is not a far-off, distant work of the Bible that goes ignored. Unlike many of the other commentaries I have done up to this point, it is not a book with an ambiguous or forgotten identity. If anything, it is an extremely common reference guide and cited and studied book. Most Christians uphold Ephesians as an important part of their faith, something with much content to imitate and to relay. We hear many sermons about marriage, about spiritual warfare and the need to be prepared, and messages about parents and children, all coming from the different passages in Ephesians. We see different passages from Ephesians on church letterheads and different banners and signs, so it is obvious that Ephesians is a book considered of importance in the faith.

This all begs one question, however: do we understand it?

In all the years I have heard various verses plucked out of Ephesians here and there, I never once made the connection between the book of Ephesians as a unit and the revelation of the church. This was even true many years after having studied it on a scholarly level, using it in preaching, and even discovering the important revelations relevant to the Ephesians 4:11 ministry, found obviously in Ephesians chapter 4. The book of Ephesians always seemed like a codebook of random ideas, things that were here, and there, and everywhere, but never truly unified.

When Sanctuary International Fellowship

Tabernacle was new, I taught weekly Bible teachings on different topics, as was my custom. I was used to topical preaching and teaching because, for the duration of my ministry, that was mostly how I taught and preached. I saved commentaries and verse-by-verse teaching for writing and college classes. But a few weeks in, I was looking up something for a topical teaching when the Lord revealed to me, "The book of Ephesians is about the church." I had never thought of Ephesians like this, and the more I studied the book for the Sunday teachings, the more I could see exactly what the Lord had spoken to me. Ephesians, in all six chapters, was about the church. Any time we try to take Ephesians out of that context, it doesn't make sense.

Thus, even though Ephesians has been preached on, written on, contemplated, and analyzed repeatedly, I write the commentary revelation that God gave me for the book of Ephesians. Much of this, plus some, was taught in our first Bible book contextual study over a six-week period at Sanctuary Apostolic Fellowship (now Sanctuary International Fellowship Tabernacle) in Raleigh, North Carolina, starting in November 2015 and ending in December 2015. Studying the specific book in this light gave us great insight into so many dimensions and aspects of the church we frequently overlook, or fail to see: that the church has always been a part of the plan of God, that by being a part of the church, we are a part of something eternal, and that God can use even the most ordinary and mundane aspects of our lives to teach something powerful in the spiritual realm and walk as a living type to Him.

It's great to have our favorite books, areas of Scripture that we repeatedly study throughout our lives, and even passages that get us through difficult times and help take us to new places in Christ. It is important, however, that we understand the passages we are reading, and we see them in a larger and eternal context, one which connects us to God in everything that we encounter in our lives. It is also important that we see ourselves connected to the church, as the church is a vital part of our spiritual growth and development. If we want to be a part of Christ beyond just a relationship, but a part of His living body, we must be a part of the church. The church, both universal and local, both corporeal and spiritual, is an entity to which we should rejoice and celebrate our participation within, never scorning or rejecting it, but with full assurance, walking in grace unto salvation all the days of our lives.

Here we shall look at Ephesians with new eyes and hearts, open minds and open ideals. We shall see our beloved church, the Bride of Christ, living and partnering with Him this side of heaven. In the very life of our church, we are a part of that which is ancient, that which is futuristic, that which is now, that which is eternal, that which is ordinary, and that which is extraordinary. It gives meaning to our lives, our relationships, the work we must do, the problems and tasks we face in life, and above all, gives us hope for what is to come. In the church, we see Jesus, living and active with us, calling us, engaging us, married to us. We are His Body, and He is the One Who created, sustained, died, and humbled Himself, that we might be free. Here, we are one; we are redeemed; we are His. If He were to never do another thing for any of us, the church is here to remind us that He has done enough...and in His grace...He is still not done with us.

Introduction

About the Book of Ephesians

The church: past, present, forever, and most of all, every day, are all fascinating subjects for the believer. Even with all the preaching and teaching done on the book of Ephesians, have you considered how much of the church is present in its few chapters? In our study on the book of Ephesians, you will note the following key points:

- The church has always been a part of God's plan, from before the founding of the world.

- Our participation in the church has always been a part of God's plan, and God knew that we would be a part of this plan, before we were ever born.

- The corporate body of the church, present with believers from everywhere in the world, brought together to become a part of this living, breathing Kingdom of God, working here on earth and changing lives with the message of salvation, every day.

- The church, no matter how many are in it or how different those in it may be, are one in Christ.

- The grace that is present in the church, especially working in the office of the apostle.

- The essential beliefs of the church.

- The leadership needed to further the work of the church in apostles, prophets, evangelists, pastors, and teachers.

- The essentials of everyday life and living, both among those who are in the church and those who are in the world.

- Seeing the mysteries of the church, things that we cannot fathom with our natural minds, in the everyday, ordinary things we encounter, including marriage.

- Recognizing God cares about the everyday and ordinary aspects of our lives.

- Seeing the spiritual answers to dealing with worldly problems, including spiritual warfare.

Position in the Bible

The book of Ephesians is a part of the New Testament epistles (a word meaning "letters"), written by the Apostle Paul. It is preceded by the book of Galatians and is followed by the book of Philippians.

Length

The book of Ephesians is six chapters. Even in Bibles that sometimes number the verses differently, there is no alteration in the numeration of Ephesians, and Ephesians always remains a six-chapter book.

Author

The book of Ephesians was written, according to

traditional understanding, by the Apostle Paul. There are some who believe the book may have been written as pseudepigrapha: in the name of the Apostle Paul, but possibly by someone else who was strongly influenced by his teaching and ministry. Either way, the thoughts of the Apostle Paul heavily inspire and drive the contents of this book.

About the author

We are familiar with the Apostle Paul as the New Testament "apostle to the Gentiles." As both a Roman citizen by birth and a Jew, the Apostle Paul was in a unique position after his conversion to reach out to audiences that were both Jewish and Gentile. He was originally noted as Saul of Tarsus, a Pharisee who was zealously opposed to the Gospel and advancement of the church. He sought out and persecuted Christians to the ultimate degree, until a trip to Damascus changed his life. On the way, Jesus called out to him in a vision, and from that vision, Saul became a Christian. For a period of fifteen years, he trained for ministry before going out and serving as an apostle of the Lord, working among non-Jewish communities to establish churches and to help in the development of the church. He went on at least three missionary journeys and appears to have spent his final years in Rome, as a prisoner. We do not know for certain how the Apostle Paul died, although traditional sources cite he was martyred for his faith during the reign of Nero.

Time written

The book of Ephesians was most likely written during the Apostle Paul's first imprisonment in Rome, somewhere around 62 AD. Some feel the authorship may have been later, somewhere between 70 to 80 AD.

Who is Ephesians for?

The book of Ephesians was written not as a book, but as a letter, to the church in Ephesus. The church at Ephesus (also mentioned in the book of Revelation) was an ancient Greek city known for the Temple of Artemis and was the third largest city of Roman Asia Minor. From this city, the Gospel spread all through the Roman province of Asia. This means that the book of Ephesians was literally for an important seat of faith in the ancient world, and is of equal relevance for us, the church, right now, in understanding who the church is and the purpose of the church in the world. It is for every believer, to understand its purpose as well as their purpose, in connection with God's eternal plan.

History

The early church was about as colorful and diverse as the church is today. People disagreed on how to get things done, people disagreed on what was supposed to happen, and they disagreed on how to get the church to function. As a strictly Greek city with strong Roman influences due to Roman capture, Ephesus was noted for its uniquely pagan culture, its large open-air theater used for drama and gladiator combats and conquests, and many public advances for its time, including bath complexes and aqueduct systems. Rome ruled much of the ancient world, despite Rome burning around 64 AD, and the fall of Jerusalem in 70 AD. It was a time of intense change as the church grew up and flourished, pinpointing many different trade routes and merchant's routes to spread and proclaim the Gospel.

Context

The book of Ephesians gives us deep insight into the church and into how much God loves the church and loves those who are His, who are a part of it. We see the

Apostle Paul delve into the deeply spiritual aspects of the church in connection with creation, the bigger plan of God, and about becoming more than just people who have faith, but truly are believers. God reveals to us the connection between being a believer and being a part of the church, why being a part of the church is important for all believers, and on how much God cares for the church. Ephesians shows us an angle of the fatherhood of God that we don't often consider, and that is His true care and nurture for His people, seeing everything as a part of a bigger plan and purpose, and seeing ourselves as a part of this great plan, even in the ordinary, mundane parts of our lives.

Chapter One

THE PLAN OF THE CHURCH (EPHESIANS CHAPTER 1)

Key verses

- **Verses 4-6:** *For He chose us in Him before the creation of the world to be holy and blameless in His sight. In love He predestined us to be adopted as His sons through Jesus Christ, in accordance with His pleasure and will – to the praise of His glorious grace, which He has freely given us in the One He loves.*

- **Verses 11-13:** *In Him we were also chosen, having been predestined according to the plan of Him Who works out everything in conformity with the purpose of His will, in order that we, who were the first to hope in Christ, might be for the praise of His glory. And you also were included in Christ when you heard the word of truth, the Gospel of your salvation. Having believed, you were marked in Him with a seal, the promised Holy Spirit.*

- **Verse 17:** *I keep asking that the God of our Lord Jesus Christ, the glorious Father, may give you the Spirit of wisdom and revelation, so that you may know Him better.*

- **Verses 22-23:** *And God placed all things under His feet and appointed Him to be head over everything for the church, which is His body, the fullness of Him Who fills everything in every way.*

Words and phrases to know

- **Paul:** From the Greek word *Paulos* which means "Paul or Paulus = "small or little." Paul was the most famous of the apostles and wrote a good part of the NT, the 14 Pauline epistles."[1]

- **Will:** From the Greek word *thelema* which means "what one wishes or has determined shall be done; will, choice, inclination, desire, pleasure."[2]

- **Saints:** From the Greek word *hagios* which means "most holy thing, a saint."[3]

- **Ephesus:** From the Greek word *Ephesos* which means "Ephesus = "permitted." a maritime city of Asia Minor, capital of Ionia and under the Romans, of proconsular Asia, situated on the Icarian Sea between Smyrna and Miletus."[4]

- **Faithful:** From the Greek word *pistos* which means "trusty, faithful; of persons who show themselves faithful in the transaction of business, the execution of commands, or the discharge of official duties; easily persuaded."[5]

- **Grace:** From the Greek word *charis* which means "grace; good will, loving-kindness, favour; what is due to grace; thanks, (for benefits, services, favours), recompense, reward."[6]

- **Peace:** From the Greek word *eirene* which means "a state of national tranquility; peace between individuals, i.e. harmony, concord; security, safety, prosperity, felicity, (because peace and harmony make and keep things safe and prosperous); of the Messiah's peace; of Christianity, the tranquil state of a soul assured of its salvation through Christ, and so fearing nothing from God and content with its earthly lot, of whatsoever sort that is; the blessed state of devout and upright men after death."[7]

- **Praise:** From the Greek word *eulogetos* which means "blessed, praised."[8]

- **Blessed:** From the Hebrew word *eulogeo* which means "to praise, celebrate with praises; to invoke blessings; to consecrate a thing with solemn prayers; of God."[9]

- **Heavenly realms:** From the Greek word *epouranios* which means "existing in heaven; of heavenly origin or nature."[10]

- **Chose:** From the Greek word *eklegomai* which means "to pick out, choose, to pick or choose out for oneself."[11]

- **Before:** From the Greek word *pro* which means, "before."[12]

- **Creation of the world:** From two Greek words: *katabole* which means "a throwing or laying down; a founding (laying down a foundation)"[13] and *kosmos* which means "an apt and harmonious arrangement or constitution, order, government; ornament, decoration, adornment, i.e. the arrangement of the stars, 'the heavenly hosts', as the ornament of the heavens. 1 Pet. 3:3 3) the world, the universe; the circle of the earth, the earth; the inhabitants of the earth, men, the human race; the ungodly multitude; the whole mass of men alienated from God, and therefore hostile to the cause of Christ; world affairs, the aggregate of things earthly; any aggregate or general collection of particulars of any sort."[14]

- **Holy:** From the Greek word *hagios* which means "most holy thing, a saint."[15]

- **Blameless:** From the Greek word *amomos* which means "without blemish; morally: without blemish, faultless, unblameable."[16]

- **Love:** From the Greek word *agape* which means "brotherly love, affection, good will, love, benevolence; love feasts."[17]

- **Predestined:** From the Greek word *proorizo* which means "to predetermine, decide beforehand; in the NT of God decreeing from eternity; to foreordain, appoint beforehand."[18]

- **Adopted:** From the Greek word *huiothesia* which means "adoption, adoption as sons."[19]

- **Redemption:** From the Greek word *apolutrosis* which means "a releasing effected by payment of ransom."[20]

- **Forgiveness:** From the Greek word *aphesis* which means "release from bondage or imprisonment; forgiveness or pardon, of sins (letting them go as if they had never been committed), remission of the penalty."[21]

- **Riches:** From the Greek word *ploutos* which means "riches, wealth."[22]

- **Wisdom:** From the Greek word *sophia* which means "wisdom, broad and full of intelligence; used of the knowledge of very diverse matters."[23]

- **Understanding:** From the Greek word *phronesis* which means "understanding; knowledge and holy love of the will of God."[24]

- **Fulfillment:** From the Greek word *pleroma* which means "that which is (has been) filled; that which fills or with which a thing is filled; fulness, abundance; a fulfilling, keeping."[25]

- **Gospel:** From the Greek word *euaggelion* which means "a reward for good tidings; good tidings."[26]

- **Salvation:** From the Greek word *soteria* which means "deliverance, preservation, safety, salvation; salvation as the present possession of all true Christians; future salvation, the sum of benefits and blessings which the Christians, redeemed from all earthly ills, will enjoy after the visible return of Christ from heaven in the consummated and eternal kingdom of God."[27]

- **Inheritance:** From the Greek word *kleronomia* which means "an inheritance, property received (or to be received) by inheritance; what is given to one as a possession."[28]

- **Faith:** From the Greek word *pistis* which means "conviction of the truth of anything, belief; in the NT of a conviction or belief respecting man's relationship to God and divine things, generally with the included idea of trust and holy fervour born of faith and joined with it; fidelity, faithfulness."[29]

- **Enlightened:** From the Greek word *photizo* which means "to give light, to shine; to enlighten, light up, illumine; to bring to light, render evident; to enlighten, spiritually, imbue with saving knowledge."[30]

- **Hope:** From the Greek word *elpis* which means "expectation of evil, fear; expectation of good, hope; on hope, in hope, having hope."[31]

- **Strength:** From the Greek word *ischus* which means "ability, force, strength, might."[32]

Ephesians 1:1-2

Paul, an apostle of Christ Jesus by the will of God,
To the saints in Ephesus, the faithful in Christ Jesus:
Grace and peace to you from God our Father and the Lord Jesus Christ.

(Related Bible references: Romans 1:1, Romans 1:5, 1 Corinthians 1:1, 1 Corinthians 4:1-13, 1 Corinthians 9:1-27, 2 Corinthians 1:1)

The city of Ephesus was located on the coast of Ionia, in what is present-day Turkey. It was a city deeply entrenched in its own unique flavor of Greek culture, influenced by the Temple of Artemis. That temple had been in place so long, it was noted for goddess worship throughout the region.

It was also deeply affected by the Roman invasion. Their tightly knit, culturally Greek world never quite made the leap to Roman society. The more Rome invaded, the more these local citizens embraced their Greek identities (even unto the persecution of Latin-speaking people). It was in this world, one marred by the rise and fall of nations, struggling to maintain its changing identity, and mixed with ancient pagan beliefs, that Ephesus – a church influenced by both the

Apostles John and Peter – rose to influence the people of near Asia.

None of these factors came together by accident. It's not an accident that the church flourished in a society fighting for tradition while on the cusp of change. This sounds much like the work of the church throughout the ages. As Christians, we find ourselves constantly challenged by the world in which we live. As the world struggles, it holds on to traditions in the hopes it can avoid the inevitable change that's part of societal transition. From age to age, the church finds itself somewhere in between tradition and progress, learning just where it fits best to usher its own divine change.

As I addressed in the introduction, the book of Ephesians was not written as a "book" like we understand it today. It was written as a letter, not divided into chapters and verses, but all written together for public reading at the church in Ephesus. The Apostle Paul and the church at Ephesus were in regular contact via letters and wrote Ephesians to continue that communication. In the bigger picture, this means all the New Testament epistles were part of an ongoing conversation, something that addressed concerns, insights, information, and praises and disciplines going on within those congregations. When we look at the Biblical epistles in this light, it is quite amazing to think we are reading part of a conversation, a discussion that has become so notable, it is lasting down through the generations. We are receiving insight and divine guidance from a conversation that was had nearly 2,000 years ago.

This means, as a conversation, we don't know the Ephesian church's response. We don't know what they asked for further clarification about, what they didn't quite understand, or what they wanted to know more about. It's hard to read Ephesians and imagine someone complaining about its contents, but it is very possible. For this reason, the Apostle Paul started his letters by affirming who he was in Christ, an apostle by the will of

God. There was no question as to his position in the church. He didn't feel it necessary to do the work of an apostle without the title and was quick to remind the church exactly who he was. This wasn't just an ordinary letter, but one that established structure, answered questions, dealt with doctrinal and theological points, and taught on essential things of faith. It was a letter that was written with authority, an authority that was given of God, and not of mankind. That authority was within the will of God, something that came from God Himself, not from the structure and teachings of men.

This tells us some important things about the office of the apostle, if for no other reason, than for our own edification. In this one sentence, we learn the following about the apostle:

- The apostle is an apostle of Jesus Christ, not of another god, another messenger, or of another prophet (Romans 1:1, 1 Corinthians 1:1).

- The apostle is sent with the divine message, namely the Gospel of Christ. More specifically in relationship to that, they are sent with the mysteries of the church, as we shall see as we go along in this book (Romans 1:5).

- The apostolic office exists by the will of God. It is not something that is fabricated or made up, but something that exists on purpose, deliberately, and in God's time (1 Corinthians 4:1-13).

- The apostle, by the will of God, discusses and reveals that will to those who are faithful in Christ Jesus (1 Corinthians 9:1-27).

The Apostle Paul makes it clear to whom this letter is for: it is for the saints, the church, the faithful who believe in Jesus Christ. It's not a letter for the world, something to use to gain the favor or attention of the world. Those of the world might understand portions of it, but overall, don't grasp the complexities of faith present in this letter. While Ephesians definitely holds important insights for anyone who wants to learn more about the church, it is certainly not something that a person who has not been transformed by Christ will fully understand.

So, what does it mean to be believers? I have been noticing many stories from overseas about people of faith in different parts of the world. I'll hear about incidents where the leaders tell the women in the church to leave their underwear at home so "God" can enter them while at service, about pastors who drown in front of their congregations while trying to walk on water, and leaders who want to baptize people in bleach to make them "white as snow." These things are done by people who have faith, and quite literal faith, at that. They believe they can do and be and speak just as people did in the Bible, without hesitation or question. Yet, we read their responses and can't believe anyone would do these things or fall for some of the stuff that people try to pull. It confounds and inspires at the same time.

This is an example of faith without true belief. These people believe, but they have never learned to give context to their faith. People who pursue such nonsense might believe anything is possible but haven't learned how to understand faith in an everyday context, where the Bible becomes a truly living word, something to apply to everyday circumstances and to understand in a context from eternity past to eternity future. If we are going to be believers, we need to have a good sense of what it means to be a part of the church, to be in the church and to be a part of this great eternity right here and now.

This letter, its contents, and its revelation are sent to those who shall read it with grace and peace, receiving unmerited favor and complete wholeness and balance, which comes from God our Father and the Lord

Jesus Christ. It's not sent in hostility or anger, nor is it sent with threat or intimidation. It is sent from one believer with the revelation and authority to deliver it to other believers, each one precious to God and ready to understand what God desires them to know. God cares about all of us, and our whole beings, that we might be made complete as we are transformed by Him, as part of His church in His wondrous design and purpose.

Ephesians 1:3-10

Praise be to the God and Father of our Lord Jesus Christ, Who has blessed us in the heavenly realms with every spiritual blessing in Christ. For He chose us in Him before the creation of the world to be holy and blameless in His sight. In love He predestined us to be adopted as His sons through Jesus Christ, in accordance with His pleasure and will – to the praise of His glorious grace, which He has freely given us in the One He loves. In Him we have redemption through His blood, the forgiveness of sins, in accordance with the riches of God's grace that He lavished on us with all wisdom and understanding. And He made known to us the mystery of His will according to His good pleasure, which He purposed in Christ, to be put into effect when the times will have reached their fulfillment – to bring all things in heaven and on earth together under one head, even Christ.

(Related Bible references: Psalm 1:1-3, Isaiah 43:21, Jeremiah 16:1-2, Ezekiel 4:1-12, Hosea 1:1-11, Matthew 1:18-25, Luke 1:26-38, John 1:16, John 3:16-17, John 17:24, Acts 10:1-48, Acts 13:38, Romans 3:25, Romans 15:14-22, Romans 12:4-8, 1 Corinthians 12:1-11, 1 Corinthians 12:12-31, 1 Corinthians 13:10-12, Galatians 3:14, Galatians 5:22-23, Ephesians 4:11, Colossians 1:14-23, Colossians 2:13, 2 Thessalonians 2:13, 2 Timothy 1:9, Titus 2:11-14, Hebrews 10:24-25, Hebrews 12:1-3, 1 Peter 1:20, 1 Peter 2:1-25, 2 Peter 3:18, Jude 1:1, Revelation 5:9).

God has given to us, in so many ways, that we cannot

fathom as a part of His created order. It is God's pleasure to give and give above and beyond what we might expect. He has given us this earth to embrace and care for, He has given to us His revelation, He has given us His Word, and above all, He has given us His Son. It is unfathomable that God would even think to give us something more than we have already received.

What, then, does it mean to be blessed with a "spiritual blessing?" It means God has given us something that natural order cannot take away. It comes from above, touching us beyond the material realm. Though we are here, we experience all God has and is from up above. They are powerful encounters we have with eternity, reminding us that no matter how much or how little we have this side of heaven, this isn't all there is.

With the prosperity movement in many churches, people believe the only way God blesses them is with what they can see. They go from thing to thing, looking for the next item to receive, the next thing to believe for, so they can receive their "reward" for being a believer. Rather than thinking they've received divine favor by profitable weather, crops, or "good luck," they think it comes through material things. It is as if too many leaders are endorsing a "Santa Claus" mentality to spiritual things: if you are very, very good, then God will reward you for what you have done, and you will get something material in exchange for being good.

Obviously, this mentality is a problem. It creates a bartering system in the minds of people, much like we see among ancient pagan systems. The spiritual world returns through material goods or with things that people want and expect God to materialize for them. For example: I have met many women, especially the past few years, who exemplify what we would classify as "holy" values. They are following what they believe to be a God-mandated lifestyle for single women: they refrain from dating; they aren't sexually active; and are "focused" on the things of God. The problem is, they do it with the intention that by doing so, God will give them the husband they desire. It is not acceptable to just have any husband, but a husband that will meet all their specifications, requirements, dreams, and hopes, all in the form of one perfect man.

This sounds great on the surface – Obey God and He'll do everything you want, any time. The problem with it is that it doesn't happen. If we are so busy looking for what we want to manifest, we are missing what God might be trying to teach us through different things in our lives. In our pursuit of what we want, we are missing the spiritual blessings He tries to present to us. Sometimes God asks things of us to teach not just us, but others, as well; things we can't value this side of heaven, and these things don't always feel so great. Throughout Bible history, there are so many examples of people who had to do things that maybe they didn't like or maybe didn't agree with. What God asks of those He has called and chosen is often difficult, and the reward is often, in and of itself, nothing more than simple obedience. Examples include:

- Hosea being told to marry a prostitute and have children by her (Hosea 1:1-11).

- Ezekiel being asked to eat and lay in his own excrement for long periods of time (Ezekiel 4:1-12).

- Mary being asked to be the mother of Jesus, thus leaving her unmarried and pregnant (Luke 1:26-38).

- Joseph being asked to marry Mary, even though she was pregnant with a child that was not his (Matthew 1:18-25).

- The Apostles Peter and Paul's calls to go to the Gentiles (Acts 10:1-48, Romans 15:14-22).

None of these individuals would have jumped at the idea of doing any of these things for the Lord. They all contradicted everything they were told the law was about and represented undesirable things that would have made them undesirable before others. They risked reputations, ideals, thoughts, and concepts that people had about God. In their very lives, they had to do things that were hard for them. Obeying God didn't reap them everything they wanted in life. What it did do, however, was bring them to a place of obedience, one where they saw things in a different perspective and were able to get spiritual insight. The ultimate spiritual blessing is the ability to love as God loves, and we learn that as we are a part of the church. In our pursuit to get there, God has given us many other spiritual blessings that have no earthly value but are beyond irreplaceable. Some of these spiritual blessings include:

- **Salvation** (John 3:16-17)

- **The spiritual gifts:** Word of wisdom, word of knowledge, faith, healing, miracles, prophecy, discernment of spirits, speaking in tongues, interpretation of tongues, service (ministry), teaching, edification, giving (mercy), leading (1 Corinthians 12:1-11, Romans 12:4-8).

- **The five-fold ministry gifts:** Apostle, prophet, evangelist, pastor, and teacher (Ephesians 4:11). We shall discuss these more in chapters 3 and 4.

- **The fruit of the Spirit:** Love, joy, peace, patience, kindness, goodness, faithfulness, gentleness (humility) and self-control (Galatians 5:22-23).

- **Spiritual growth** (Psalm 1:1-3, 1 Corinthians 13:10-12, Titus 2:11-14, Hebrews 10:24, 1 Peter 2:1-25, 2 Peter 3:18).

All these spiritual blessings cost something from us. They cause us to grow, to examine life from a different angle than we have before. They are disciplinary tools that make it so living right isn't this extraordinary task, but something we are able to tackle in every situation. God has given us this amazing ability to know Him, to come before Him and learn from Him, receiving every promise that He has for us, with nothing lacking. We are here, a part of this work, to be holy, to be blameless, and to be a part of the church without spot or wrinkle.

When we become a part of the church, we become a part of eternity. It is this eternal picture that should be the focus of every believer, which is why spiritual blessings are so important and so key to our faith development and understanding. Spiritual blessings are something we reap in eternity, and eternity is not something that just starts when we die. Eternal life is eternal life, and that means it is a part of our right now as much as it will be later in time. God wants us to see ourselves as a part of this bigger picture, a perspective and thought process that is bigger than right now, today or tomorrow. It's bigger than our finances, our wants, hopes, and dreams, and spiritual blessings are a part of that. We understand them as we understand eternity more and more, one step at a time.

For this reason, it is important we understand spiritual blessings in a deep way. We must also understand spiritual blessings as a part of the church and the church's history. The spiritual blessings God gives to us are blessings that believers have received all throughout history. If we look at church history, it helps us better understand what God has in store for each of us.

Have you, as a Christian, ever wondered about the history of the church? When I talk about church history, I am not just talking about the history of Christianity this side of heaven, discussing the ins and outs of the past 2,000 years. Yes, the history of the church on the earth and its varying ins and outs, denominations, workings, changes, and even driftings, are all a part of what has made the church a viable working body for all this time. It is important to see the church this side of heaven, and the people who have built it up. But many people do not consider that the history of the church did not just start 2,000 years ago. We read here in Ephesians 1 that the Lord blessed us in the heavenly realms with every spiritual blessing, choosing us in Him before the creation of the world. The existence of the church has been a part of God's plan since the beginning, since before the foundations of the world, and since that time, God knew that we would be a part of that amazing process, that amazing plan that has existed forever and ever (Hebrews 12:1-3).

The existence of the church did not just happen by accident. If we read history, it teaches the church exists because people of like minds needed somewhere to gather to support one another and encourage growth. This is not, in and of itself, completely unfounded. It is true that in the natural realm, the church evolved for this reason. The Bible itself specifies that it is good for us to meet together, and that we should not forsake our assembly (Hebrews 10:25). At the same time, however, being a part of the church is about something much bigger and something much more important. Thus, being a part of the church is an essential – and inescapable part – of being a believer. Yes, it is awesome to have a relationship with God for oneself and yes, all of us need to have that. This does not nullify us, however, from being a part of the church. It is through the church that we touch eternity and that our relationship with God can remain balanced and healthy. Our own relationship with God was never meant to isolate us from other believers, or to keep us in a position where we believe everything we want is from God, thus we never have any accountability. Our personal relationship with God is just that – a personal relationship – to help us learn to hear the voice of God in our own lives and develop the needed characteristics and depth to walk in obedience throughout our lives.

We became a part of the church, also called the body of Christ (1 Corinthians 12:12-31), when we were born again in Christ, and recognizing God's plan in the church from eternity past to eternity future means we are not here by accident. Referring to the church as the "body of Christ" means the church is a living, breathing, existing, participating, growing, and mutual group of believers who are in Christ, working as His hands and feet to the world. It's our job to bring eternity down to the level of this world, to a level people who don't know the Lord can understand, doing His work. That is why we aren't removed from this earth. Through us, eternity becomes tangible. Eternity needs to touch the world we are in, and God chooses all of us to do it. We are His people, the people who know Him and have heard His voice, and we realize that Jesus Christ is our originator, our head, and in Him, we have every spiritual blessing (Colossians 1:15-23).

Belonging to this eternal church is about far more than just signing a roster or finding a church to attend when you move to a city. We have been redeemed, bought with Christ's blood, brought to a new place in Him. Just as in ancient cultures when we would talk about the concept of a dowry and a man paying a large sum of money to marry a woman, Christ bought us with His own blood, according to the ancient system. The most precious thing any being could give for any other being is their own life, and that is exactly what Christ has done for us. By blood, we have been brought into eternity, the ultimate sacrifice for sin made, in the place where we can find forgiveness and hope. Those riches, those spiritual blessings, are perceived to us by knowledge and understanding, which only He can give to us. They are not always things we can see and touch, but we know they are there as we have the assurance that God is working within us, for us, and through us.

The will of God is, in the eyes of history and to many even now, a great mystery. Many are perplexed at the concept that we can know what God wills for us and understand it in any semblance within our lives. It seems mystifying to us because we have not learned to understand the ways that God makes His messages known. We learn from Ephesians that God's ultimate revelation is made known in Christ in the fulfillment of all times, when Jesus shall return and set all things in order. This doesn't mean that God doesn't reveal things to us in the meantime, however. Every word, every understanding, every development we have as we go along in this spiritual life has a time and a season. One thing is fulfilled, and we understand it better. One word comes to pass, and we see the manifestation as we learn from it. In everything we do, there is a fulfillment, a seedtime and a harvest time, and God reveals to us the depths of His mysteries, those set in eternity, to us who have gone beyond the natural and put on the spiritual.

Ephesians 1:11-14

In Him we were also chosen, having been predestined according to the plan of Him Who works out everything in conformity with the purpose of His will, in order that we, who were the first to hope in Christ, might be for the praise of His glory. And you also were included in Christ when you heard the word of truth, the Gospel of your salvation. Having believed, you were marked in Him with a seal, the promised Holy Spirit, Who is a deposit guaranteeing our inheritance until the redemption of those who are God's possession – to the praise of His glory.

(Related Bible references: Genesis 3:15-16, Isaiah 46:10, Romans 8:17, 2 Corinthians 1:22, 2 Corinthians 5:5, Galatians 3:2, Ephesians 5:21-33, 1 Timothy 2:4-6, James 1:18)

Different religious denominations interpret this passage in different ways. Unfortunately, many of them understand it in a way that is exclusive, cold, hard to understand, and even harder to embrace. The problem is many don't read it properly and can't figure out exactly what is being "predestined" in the words of the apostle. Is it the people, is it the church, is it God's work, what is it?

As people, God knew we would be a part of His eternal plan before the foundations of the world. That does not mean, however, that we are the only people God desires to be saved, or to know salvation. It is not us that is predestined as individual people, but the plan of God, the work of the church which has existed forever. God knew Adam and Eve would sin before they were ever created. God's plan for the salvation of the world was bigger than just you or me. God knew that we would belong to Him, and be a part of His plan, but it doesn't mean that only a small, elect group of people can come to know Him and be saved. Salvation is open to anyone who shall receive, and who shall willingly come and be a part of this plan, this eternity, that we have within Him and Him alone. In the church, it is our place to focus on that plan, and on heralding that plan to others who shall too come to be a part of this plan.

Genesis 3:15-16:

I will make you and the woman
enemies to each other [place hostility/enmity between you and the woman].
Your descendants [seed] and her descendants [seed]
will be enemies.
One of her descendants [He] will crush your head,
and you will bite [strike; bruise; crush] His heel [Rom. 16:20; Rev. 12:9]."

Then God said to the woman,
"I will cause you to have much trouble [or increase your pain]
when you are pregnant [in childbearing],
and when you give birth to children,

you will have great pain.
You will greatly desire [the word implies a desire to control; 4:7] your husband,
but he will rule over you." (EXB)

This prophecy, more than any other specified passage in the early chapters of Genesis, proves the plan of the church was always present within the mind and plan of God. While humanity has officially moved into sin, both Adam and Eve moving away from God via sin and deception, God made a promise to Eve and to all who would come after her. God was not going to leave humanity in a lost state, alienated from Him. God had a better plan, a better purpose, something more incredible to unite all of us to than just a man and woman in paradise. The prophecy reveals a few key things to us about the church, because as with many Biblical prophecies, she is hiding in the words of the text:

- **The woman and the serpent are automatic enemies from this point on:** All that is represented within the woman, and those who are the descendants of this woman, have an automatic response to evil and to manipulation. The hostility placed there, often instinctual in women, is God-given.

- **The descendants of the woman are automatic enemies with the serpent:** I shall discuss this in detail paralleling with the next point.

- **One descendant shall come from the woman, who shall be begotten without the assistance of a natural man, the "seed" of a woman:** Biology tells us it takes a biological male and female to create life, with the man offering seed. This prophecy speaks of a child's birth from the seed of a woman, Who will crush the head (or authority) of the enemy, and the enemy shall bruise His heel. We know this to be a prophecy of the birth, death, and resurrection of Jesus Christ, all in a few words. By His birth, Jesus would be born via a divine conception that did not involve a man; by His death, the serpent struck the heel of Christ, bruising or wounding Him; by His resurrection, Christ crushed the head of the serpent, destroying his power, influence, and authority.

- **The woman, Eve, here is not just a representation of women, but of the church as well:** The type present here is not just of Eve as a woman, but Eve as a prefigure of the church to come. The church herself is feminine, as was Eve. Even though those in the church may be beguiled and charmed by Satan, the ultimate authority goes to her new Adam, Christ, because the church is the new Eve. Her descendants, those that are produced by the church, fight the battle and war with Satan, experiencing the intense odds and occasional bruising attacks that he brings our way. The ultimate victory, however, shall belong to the descendants (the church members).

- **The labor of the church shall be difficult:** The term "labor" here does not exclusively imply childbirth in the original Hebrew language. It is automatically associated with birth, however, because it is spoken of in terms of women. The "labor" spoken of to Eve and the "work labor" spoken of to Adam are the same exact word and indicate a difficulty in life. This side of heaven, the work of the church will be difficult and will be done as a labor of love.

- **The church shall desire her husband (Christ) and He will lead and guide us:** The natural aspect of this prophecy that men would rule over women is not spoken of as the ideal relationship dynamic or of a relationship built on godly principles. Nothing in it states it's God's plan or idea. It simply states this is what would happen, and this distortion causes us to misunderstand the relationship and love the church would have with Christ. The control and confusion that has resulted from abuse of power and vying for control has caused us to miss the powerful act of submission that Christ extended toward His bride in His death on the cross. In Eve, we see the promise to come: we will desire our Lord, and He will rule in His rightful authority over the church, leading us into all truth. We see fulfillment of this teaching expounded greater in Ephesians 5:21-33.

- **Every time we do something in connection with the church, we are connected all the way back to our original roots of Adam and Eve:** In their very lives, work, and relationship, Adam and Eve show us a picture of the church. We can see its struggles, its difficulties, its challenges and temptations, and we can also see its redemption. Nothing and no one, not even the gates of hell, would overcome it. They were the first to come along, the first to teach us about the church, and the first to believe and hope for a promise that they probably didn't even understand in their lifetimes.

The church in Ephesus was among the first to hope in Christ, the first to know this prophecy in Genesis came true. Church history tells us they were the first church in Asia. We can recognize that as they were among the first, so we too are a first, here in our own right. We might not be the first Christian church on the block or in a city, but we may very well be the first believers in our families, in our neighborhoods, in many generations, among our friends, or at our workplace. We might be the first one we know who was called into ministry, or the first one who we know is really called to take our relationship with God to the next level. No matter how we spin it, each one of us as a believer is a "first" in some way in our lives. We have our first encounters with God, with spiritual things, with other believers, our firsts in spiritual milestones, and many other things that will come to us, for the first time, as we develop our walk with Him.

Because we are here to do this work and we are dealing with the challenges of our firsts, it is clearly God's desire that we come to know Him better, knowing His will in a deeper sense. We are a part of an inheritance, those who belong to God, who are sealed with the Holy Spirit, which proves that we have been set apart for Him (2 Corinthians 5:5, Galatians 3:2). This means the Holy Spirit is active today, important and relevant in our lives, still at work, still moving through gifts, still moving through the church, and still moving through us. He is as alive and active as ever, because the Holy Spirit is our promise of full inheritance, helping us embrace all that we have right now, in this moment, celebrating and rejoicing over in His glory.

Ephesians 1:15-23

For this reason, ever since I heard about your faith in the Lord Jesus and your love for all the saints, I have not stopped giving thanks for you, remembering you in my prayers. I keep asking that the God of our Lord Jesus Christ, the glorious Father, may give you the Spirit of wisdom and revelation, so that you may know Him better. I pray also that the eyes of your heart may be enlightened in order that you may know the hope to which He has called you, the riches of His glorious inheritance in the saints, and His incomparably great power for us who believe. That power is like the working of His mighty strength, which He

exerted in Christ when He raised Him from the dead and seated Him at His right hand in the heavenly realms, far above all rule and authority, power and dominion, and every title that can be given, not only in the present age but also in the one to come. And God placed all things under His feet and appointed Him to be head over everything for the church, which is His body, the fullness of Him Who fills everything in every way.

(Related Bible references: Deuteronomy 33:3, Psalm 8:6, Psalm 110:1, Proverbs 2:6, Matthew 28:18, 1 Corinthians 10:31, 2 Corinthians 13:4, Galatians 6:4, Philippians 2:3-4, Colossians 1:9, Colossians 1:18, Colossians 1:27, Colossians 2:10, Colossians 3:23, 2 Thessalonians 1:3, Hebrews 7:26, Hebrews 12:2, James 5:16, 1 Peter 1:3, 1 Peter 3:22)

As believers, it should be our good pleasure to celebrate one another, remember one another, pray for one another, and edify one another (2 Thessalonians 1:3, James 5:16). We have faith in Jesus Christ, Who has brought us to this place, this eternal plan. We should always seek, and pray for others in the church, to have a deeper sense of God's wisdom and revelation. Having visions and dreams is wonderful, but it is better that we understand the ones that we have than seek them when we don't understand. If we are receiving something from God, we should have a means to have some understanding of it, even if that understanding, at present, is only in part.

This is why competition in the body is such a bad thing (Galatians 6:4, Philippians 2:3-4, Colossians 3:23). We should seek to celebrate one another and for better understanding among the body because we are all connected, and we need the gifts and abilities that we all must become something greater than we are as individuals. In the church, we need one another. We need to be connected so we can pull together and bring the message of salvation to the world. It takes all of us, every single one of us, doing exactly what God has called us to do (1 Corinthians 10:31). All the backbiting, anger, jealousy, and bitterness we see in ministry today cuts off the ability of each one of those works to be effective. If we can't work with one another, then we are missing something within each of us and our relationship with God that calls us to die to ourselves, becoming a part of this body and viewing one another and our abilities in the light of eternity.

God has given each one of us the power to be believers, as we spoke of earlier in this chapter. It is passing from faith that just believes God can do anything to believing in God in a way that changes each and every one of us into a greater sense of His image. As the light of the world, Christ illuminates our hearts and reveals to us a deeper sense of exactly Who He is, and who we are in Him. We see the same power of God that rose Christ from the dead at work in us, bringing us to a profound place where we can see ourselves and what we go through as more than just a going through and getting over. Jesus Christ rose from the dead. He wasn't reincarnated, to continue cycles; His overcoming of death broke every death cycle present within our lives and within this world. He didn't become an ascended master, who represents something that everyone can achieve by meditating and looking within. Jesus wasn't just a nice, smart guy. He is the Firstborn of the dead, the first one of all firsts, Who is seated at the right hand of God, the position of authority in heaven, with ability to rule forever and ever (Hebrews 12:2, 1 Peter 3:22). As we are found in Him, we find our fullness; our *shalom*, perfect completion, representing balance, wholeness, and the promise of all that is to come.

If Christ is the head over the church, and we are His body, then the church should be full of Christ (Colossians 1:18). Jesus should be the center, emanating from every word, every message, every action. The love of Christ should fill our hearts for this generation right now, for those we know and do not know, and for future generations. The work of Christ, resembling, acting as, doing as He would do, talking as He talked, and impacting people as He did should be the main purpose and point of our lives in eternity. As a full representation of all that Jesus is, the church should be visibly seen in Him, and His work. That means all these churches that are full of weak people and those who lack enough sense and character to do what He would have them to do aren't receiving the fullness that He has to offer. The evidence? If we have His fullness, that means we have emptied ourselves of everything that is not God. We have allowed ourselves to be emptied so that He can fill us, and we can increase as He decreases. As this happens, we allow ourselves to embrace eternity in a deeper way, and we absorb it rather than becoming more willful and stubborn.

The work of the church calls us from our own existences that remain small and seemingly unimportant to an eternal call, one that connects us with the past and the future, as well as those among us in our present who have also heard the call. It's bigger than a local church, a small gathering, and each one of us as people. The more we connect, the more we see Jesus at work, and the more we are changed from glory to glory and faith to faith as we grow into the life and work as believers.

Chapter Two

THE FORM OF CHURCH PARTICIPATION (EPHESIANS CHAPTER 2)

Key verses

- **Verses 1-2:** *As for you, you were dead in your transgressions and sins, in which you used to live when you followed the ways of this world and of the ruler of the kingdom of the air, the spirit who is now at work in those who are disobedient.*

- **Verses 8-9:** *For it is by grace you have been saved, through faith – and this not from yourselves, it is the gift of God – not by works, so that no one can boast.*

- **Verses 12-15:** *Remember at that time you were separate from Christ, excluded from citizenship in Israel and foreigners to the covenants of the promise, without hope and without God in the world. But now in Christ Jesus you who once were far away have been brought near through the blood of Christ. For He Himself is our peace, Who has made the two one and has destroyed the barrier, the dividing wall of hostility, by abolishing in His flesh the law with its commandments and regulations. His purpose was to create in Himself one new man out of the two, thus making peace.*

- **Verses 19-20:** *Consequently, you are no longer foreigners and aliens, but fellow citizens with God's people and members of God's household, built on the foundation of the apostles and prophets, with Christ Jesus Himself as the chief cornerstone.*

Words and phrases to know

- **Dead:** From the Greek word *nekros* which means "properly: one that has breathed his last, lifeless; deceased, departed, one whose soul is in Hades; destitute of life, without life, inanimate; metaph. spiritually dead, destitute of force or power, inactive, inoperative."[1]

- **Transgressions:** From the Greek word *paraptoma* which means "to fall beside or near something; a lapse or deviation from truth and uprightness."[2]

- **Sins:** From the Greek word *hamartia* which means "to be without a share in, to miss the mark, to err, be mistaken, to miss or wander from the path of uprightness and honour, to do or go wrong, to wander from the law of God, violate God's law, sin; that which is done wrong, sin, an offence, a violation of the divine law in thought or in act; collectively, the complex or aggregate of sins committed either by a single person or by many."[3]

- **Prince:** From the Greek word *archon* which means "a ruler, commander, chief, leader."[4]

- **Kingdom of the air:** From two Greek words: *exousia* which means "power of choice, liberty of doing as one pleases; physical and mental power; the power of authority (influence) and of right (privilege); the power of rule or government (the power of him whose will and commands must be submitted to by others and obeyed)"[5] and *aion* which means "for ever, an unbroken age, perpetuity of time, eternity; the worlds, universe; period of time, age."[6]

- **Disobedient:** From the Greek word *apeitheia* which means "obstinacy, obstinate opposition to the divine will."[7]

- **Sinful nature:** From the Greek word *sarx* which means "flesh (the soft substance of the living body, which covers the bones and is permeated with blood) of both man and beasts; the body; a living creature (because possessed of a body of flesh) whether man or beast; the flesh, denotes mere human nature, the earthly nature of man apart from divine influence, and therefore prone to sin and opposed to God."[8]

- **Objects of wrath:** From two Greek words: *teknon* which means "offspring, children;"[9] and *orge* which means "anger, the natural disposition, temper, character; movement or agitation of the soul, impulse, desire, any violent emotion, but esp. anger; anger, wrath, indignation; anger exhibited in punishment, hence used for punishment itself."[10]

- **Mercy:** From the Greek word *eleos* which means "mercy: kindness or good will towards the miserable and the afflicted, joined with a desire to help them."[11]

- **Alive:** From the Greek word *suzoopoieo* which means "to make alive together with."[12]

- **Saved:** From the Greek word *sozo* which means "to save, keep safe and sound, to rescue from danger or destruction."[13]

- **Kindness:** From the Greek word *chrestotes* which means "moral goodness, integrity; benignity, kindness."[14]

- **Works:** From the Greek word *ergon* which means "business, employment, that which any one is occupied; any product whatever, any thing accomplished by hand, art, industry, or mind; an act, deed, thing done: the idea of working is emphasized in opp. to that which is less than work."[15]

- **Boast:** From the Greek word *kauchaomai* which means "to glory (whether with reason or without); to glory on account of a thing; to glory in a thing."[16]

- **Workmanship:** From the Greek word *poiema* which means "that which has been made; a work."[17]

- **Gentiles:** From the Greek word *ethnos* which means "a multitude (whether of men or of beasts) associated or living together; a multitude of individuals of the same nature or genus; a race, nation, people group; in the OT, foreign nations not worshipping the true God, pagans, Gentiles; Paul uses the term for Gentile Christians."[18]

- **Uncircumcised:** From the Greek word *akrobustia* which means "having the foreskin, uncircumcised; a Gentile; a condition in which the corrupt desires rooted in the flesh were not yet extinct."[19]

- **Circumcision:** From the Greek word *peritome* which means "circumcised."[20]

- **Separate:** From the Greek word *apallotrioo* which means "to alienate, estrange; to be shut out from one's fellowship and intimacy."[21]

- **Far away:** From the Greek word *makran* which means "far, a great way; far hence."[22]

- **Near:** From the Greek word *eggus* which means "near, of place and position; of time."[23]

- **Dividing wall of hostility:** From two Greek words: *mesotoichon* which means "a partition wall"[24] and *phragmos* which means "a hedge, a fence; that which separates, prevents two from coming together."[25]

- **Abolishing:** From the Greek word *katargeo* which means "to render inoperative, abolish."[26]

- **Commandments:** From the Greek word *entole* which means "an order, command, charge, precept, injunction; a commandment."[27]

- **Regulations:** From the Greek word *dogma* which means "doctrine, decree, ordinance)."[28]

- **Reconcile:** From the Greek word *apokatallasso* which means "to reconcile completely; to reconcile back again, bring back a former state of harmony."[29]

- **Access:** From the Greek word *prosagoge* which means "the act of bringing to, a moving to; access, approach."[30]

- **Foreigners:** From the Greek word *xenos* which means "a foreigner, a stranger; one who receives and entertains another hospitably."[31]

- **Aliens:** From the Greek word *paroikos* which means "dwelling near, neighboring; in the NT, a stranger, a foreigner, one who lives in a place without the right of citizenship; metaph. without citizenship in God's kingdom, one who lives on earth as a stranger, a sojourner on the earth, of Christians whose home is in heaven."[32]

- **Citizens:** From the Greek word *sumpolites* which means "possessing the same citizenship with others, a fellow citizen."[33]

- **Household:** From the Greek word *oikeios* which means "belonging to a house or family, domestic, intimate."[34]

- **Foundation:** From the Greek word *themelios* which means "laid down as a foundation, the foundation (of a building, wall, city); metaph. the foundations, beginnings, first principals."[35]

- **Chief cornerstone:** From the Greek word *akrogoniaios* which means "placed at an extreme corner, the corner foundation stone."[36]

- **Temple:** From the Greek word *naos* which means "used of the temple at Jerusalem, but only of the sacred edifice (or sanctuary) itself, consisting of the Holy place and the Holy of Holies (in classical Greek it is used of the sanctuary or cell of the temple, where the image of gold was placed which is distinguished from the whole enclosure)."[37]

- **Dwelling:** From the Greek word *katoiketerion* which means "an abode, a habitation."[38]

Ephesians 2:1-3

As for you, you were dead in your transgressions and sins, in which you used to live when you followed the ways of this world and of the ruler of the kingdom of the air, the spirit who is now at work in those who are disobedient. All of us also lived among them at one time, gratifying the cravings of our sinful nature and following its desires and thoughts. Like the rest, we were by nature objects of wrath.

(Related Bible references: Deuteronomy 4:36, Deuteronomy 8:5, Job 5:17, Proverbs 10:17, Proverbs 15:10, Zephaniah 1:17, Matthew 4:19, Matthew 11:28, Matthew 26:41, Mark 14:38, Luke 11:4, Luke 22:40, John 12:31, Romans 3:23, Romans 5:19, Romans 11:32, Romans 12:2, 1 Corinthians 11:32, 2 Corinthians 10:6, Colossians 2:13, Colossians 3:6, Hebrews 4:11, Hebrews 12:11, 1 Peter 4:6, 1 John 2:16)

If the first chapter of Ephesians was about the church as an eternal entity, then the second chapter of Ephesians is about who is a part of the church. Obviously, if the church is a part of an eternal plan, then the church must have beings that are a part of that plan. We've already discussed that believers are a part of that plan and that when we are a part of the church, we are participating in eternity. But who are the believers? What do they look like? Where do they come from? What does it all mean, and why are they there?

There are a lot of questions today as to just who can be part of the church, as well as who is part of the church right now. Different denominations, different Christians, even different individuals vary on just what makes a person a Christian and, by extension, a part of the church. We are confused on this point due to something we discussed earlier in chapter one: the fact that we too often divorce ourselves as Christians from being part of the church. The church's head is Jesus and the body is us; that means the church has both a human and a divine component. Most of us are all right with the divine component, but we trip when it comes to the human element that tests and tries our faith, even to this very day. If we are born again, if we call ourselves Christians, that makes us part of the church. It doesn't mean we will always love everything about church membership or about the people who are also attending church, but it does mean that we cannot separate ourselves from it. Even if we avoid church for years or only go on holidays, we are still a part of the church. Maybe we don't have the right regard or relationship for the church, but we are still a part of it, nonetheless. Knowing who is in the church means we must know ourselves, where we came from, and what God brought us from:

- **Every single person has sinned and offended God:** Perhaps one of the most difficult things to accept: all of us have sinned against God. No matter how hard we have tried (or may be trying at this moment), the world we live in has tempted us. We have all succumbed to that temptation at one point in time or another. Even though our sin might not seem like a big deal to us, it is a very big deal in the eyes of God (Zephaniah 1:17, Romans 3:23).

- **If we live without God in the proper way in our lives, we are living in our sins:** Another hard truth: if we aren't allowing God to lead us in the way only He can, then we are living in a state of disobedience. Let us be careful with our understanding here. There are many who believe if they have said a certain sort of prayer or exert an exterior form of conduct, they don't have to worry about any disobedience they may have.

Disobeying God in any form – when you know He expects or has told you to do something, and you don't do it – is a sin. If you aren't living according to the obedience of God, then you are living in an active state of sin, which will not lead to life (Romans 11:32, 2 Corinthians 10:6).

- **Disobedience follows the "ways of this world and the ruler of the kingdom of the air":** There is a two-fold message in this statement. The first is that the ways of the world often do not follow the ways of God (John 12:31). This is not to say we should not be socialized people, get along with other people, or be considerate of other people in this world. The generalized concept of "the world" as is often used is not a reference to specific people, but to the general system and function by which the world keeps going. It relates to politics, to aspirations in contrast with spiritual things (such as amassing wealth or job prestige), to the compromises of personal integrity, and to the confusion of priorities, whereby selfishness overtakes the welfare and good of others or of a situation (Romans 5:19, Hebrews 4:11). More than anything else, the "world" is the realm that leads, identifies, and moves us to idolatry.

- **Every person who has truly been transformed by the work of Jesus Christ within them did also live among the world and among the disobedient:** Before we were in Christ, we lived instinctually, gravitating to what we wanted to do and what was pleasurable or pleasant to us. We avoided what was uncomfortable, whether to the detriment of ourselves or others. Nobody was born sanctified from the womb. Every one of us lives with temptations, trials, and giving in to things that maybe we shouldn't have, but did (Matthew 26:41, Mark 14:38, Luke 11:4, Luke 22:40).

- **Everyone, even those in the church, have been objects of God's wrath at some point in time:** Disobedience brings correction, which means those who were disobedient were poised for the wrath, or displeasure, of God. Members of God's church aren't any better than anyone else, and they recognize that within their own lives and choices. They have done the same things, experienced the same fallings, and dealt with the same temptations that those who are not in church have, or maybe dealing with them now (Deuteronomy 4:36, Deuteronomy 8:5, Job 5:17, Proverbs 10:17, Proverbs 15:10, 1 Corinthians 11:32, Hebrews 12:11).

Breaking down this passage shows us the nature of the church, her true heart and interest, and why the church has become such a universal facet in the proclamation of the Gospel. The very nature of the church is, by what we would define, "inclusive." This means the church is not so much about who is not allowed to be a part of it, but who is allowed to be a part of it. In a more direct speech, there is no one who is, by their nature, excluded from membership in the church if they are willing to come forward, repent of their sins, and follow the ways of Christ. Nobody is too bad, too good, too perfect, or wrong for church (Matthew 4:19, Matthew 11:28). Church is not an exclusive country club that means someone must have a lot of money to join, or is barred from joining based on race, sex, or anything else about them that humans use to exclude other people. It is open to anyone who is willing to become alive, to walk away from the death of transgression and sin and join the new life present in Christ.

This sounds simple enough, but we know from many years of church experiences that human beings make church feel like a place far from inclusive. The myriads of rules, traditions, regulations, and expectations found in many churches are designed to keep people out rather than allow people in. This atmosphere is contrary to church, and stings of the trappings of legalism. While it is completely understandable that churches must have regulations to keep a certain semblance of order, the way that rules are often used in church is to make sure that anyone who is an outsider stays outside, rather than coming inside.

We've all had starting points to our faith, and there are plenty of us who can acknowledge it took more than two or three tries, prayers, intercessions, conversations, and efforts to bring us into the faith as believers. Even once we accepted the faith, there are more than plenty of us who fell back into different patterns or gave into temptations that we shouldn't have once we were in church. That's why the Apostle Paul is very clear to clarify before talking about anything else where everyone started out before they were believers in Christ. The call of the church is to walk in humility, welcoming anyone who desires to know more about this life and this walk (even to see the truth in it and give it a try) is an essential part of the work of the Gospel.

Ephesians 2:4-10

But because of His great love for us, God, Who is rich in mercy, made us alive with Christ even when we were dead in transgressions – it is by grace you have been saved. And God raised us up with Christ and seated us with Him in the heavenly realms in Christ Jesus, in order that in the coming ages He might show the incomparable riches of His grace, expressed in His kindness to us in Christ Jesus. For it is by grace you have been saved, through faith – and this not from yourselves, it is the gift of God – not by works, so that no one can boast. For we are God's workmanship, created in Christ Jesus to do good works, which God prepared in advance for us to do.

(Related Bible references: Psalm 145:9, Song of Solomon 8:6-7, Isaiah 54:10, John 1:12, John 3:36, John 6:44, Romans 3:20, Romans 4:16, Romans 5:8, Romans 6:11, Romans 10:12, 1 Corinthians 15:22, Galatians 5:15, Colossians 1:10, Colossians 2:13, Colossians 3:1, Hebrews 11:1, James 2:14-26, 1 Peter 1:4, 1 John 4:9)

Salvation is something we often like to make sound complicated and involved, when it really isn't. I think we like to make it sound hard, taxing, and complicated so that we can feel better about the works of our own hands that we would rather people pay attention to. If we can make salvation about us – we do wonderful things because we are saved, how well we remain saved, or what we do in connection with it – then the focus isn't on Jesus, but on us. In keeping with what we have learned about the church, Ephesians 2 gives us more insight into who is a part of the church. In the last section, we learned the church is made up of whosever, no matter how messy they might have been, who desire to come to know the Lord in a deeper way. This is an extension of God's incredible, great love for us. He did not have to save us, He did not have to intervene in our lives, and He does not have to help us now. God does what He does for us out of His great love.

Song of Solomon 8:6-7 says:

Put [Set] me like a seal [leaving an impression on clay, showing ownership] on your heart [inside],
like a seal on your arm [outside].
Love is as strong as death;
jealousy [or passion] is as strong [tenacious] as the grave.
Love bursts into flames [Its flame is an intense fire]
and burns like a hot fire [or a godlike flame].
Even much water cannot put out the flame of love;
floods cannot drown [flood] love.
If a man offered everything [all the wealth] in his house for love,
people would totally reject it [or he would be completely

despised]. (EXB)

In the resurrection of Christ, felt in our own salvation experience, we see and experience this passage firsthand. The love of God and true love that considers our neighbor and loves others as we love ourselves has the power to overcome everything, even death. Our ability to be saved, to be a part of the church is a divine act of mercy, one brought out of love, manifested in the form of a favor we don't deserve. What human beings deserve in their sinful state is the wrath of God, something that merits a permanent punishment. Nothing but the love of God, something that was done in great understanding and the hope that we would see that love and respond to it, is what has worked to lift us up and bring us to a different place.

For this reason, God has made us alive in Christ, even when we were dead in our sins (Romans 6:11, 1 Corinthians 15:22, Colossians 2:13, Colossians 3:1). It is by God's grace that we are saved through faith, and not of our own merits. Our salvation by grace is that which God does, not because we deserve it, but because He loves us, and it operates through our faith – our genuine conviction of what we hope for, but cannot right now, see (Hebrews 11:1). If anything, it might very well be given to us because we don't deserve it; we need it. It's not about believing for things but about believing in God beyond what we might be taught about Him, beyond our own preconceived notions, and believing beyond our conditional, changing circumstances. We are not saved because we know how to mimic traditional church behavior, or because of how we look or interact on the outside. It's not about how many chapters of the Bible that we read every day, or how many conferences we've been to in the past year. Salvation is something that God has come into our lives to do for us. Where we couldn't do it or be it ourselves, He did it for us. Not only did He save us, but He has also raised us up, above the issues and problems of this world, and seated us in a place of overcoming authority, victory, and power, with Christ Jesus, having received this incredible gift of eternal life with Him.

Eternal life and salvation are more than just about avoiding hell or alienation from God when we die. Rather than being about avoiding something bad, eternal life and salvation are about becoming something good, about changing into something deeper. It is about becoming something new, becoming something that merits an incomparable stance from before and after. We become the workmanship of God, something that is created to do good, and make change in the world in which we live. This is why the faith vs. works debate that has raged on and on in Christianity for centuries is a true diversion from what the Word desires to teach us.

James 2:14-26 tells us:

My brothers and sisters, what good does it do if someone claims to have faith but doesn't do any good things? Can this kind of faith save him? Suppose a believer, whether a man or a woman, needs clothes or food and one of you tells that person, "God be with you! Stay warm, and make sure you eat enough." If you don't provide for that person's physical needs, what good does it do? In the same way, faith by itself is dead if it doesn't cause you to do any good things.

Another person might say, "You have faith, but I do good things." Show me your faith apart from the good things you do. I will show you my faith by the good things I do. You believe that there is one God. That's fine! The demons also believe that, and they tremble with fear.

You fool! Do you have to be shown that faith which does nothing is useless? Didn't our ancestor Abraham receive God's approval as a result of what he did when he offered his son Isaac as a sacrifice on the altar? You see that Abraham's faith and what he did worked together. His faith was shown to be genuine by what he did. The Scripture passage came true. It says, "Abraham believed God, and that faith was regarded as the basis of

Abraham's approval by God." So Abraham was called God's friend. You see that a person receives God's approval because of what he does, not only because of what he believes. The same is true of the prostitute Rahab who welcomed the spies and sent them away on another road. She received God's approval because of what she did.

A body that doesn't breathe is dead. In the same way faith that does nothing is dead. (GW)

The work of the Apostle James doesn't contradict the words of the Apostle Paul. If anything, they add to one another and beautifully complement each other. The Apostle James is talking about our life of faith, while the Apostle Paul is explaining to us about the dynamics of our salvation. Our salvation is God's display to us, something that is completely not of our doing. It is something that God does within us when we have faith and let Him develop things deeper within us. Our works are the product of everything that we do as we are guided by our faith, and everything that we do should match the transformation that is going on inside of us.

I have met many a professing Christian who claim to be transformed but act the same as they always have. I have met people who claim to be redeemed, but are angry, cantankerous, and sour. The largest group I have met, however, are those who claim to be Christians, but do nothing. They might have many opinions, they might be quite vocal about what is wrong with the world, but they sit back and do nothing. They do nothing to live their faith, to live in love for others in a way that has the power to transform. The world never changed from anyone's opinions about it. If we are a changed people, then our change needs to be apparent. The only way that happens is if we show that we have become different through our works. With an inclusive church goes being an active and involved church.

Those good works that we do show the world that there is something different about us, about what we are doing, and most importantly, about the God that we serve, Who has stepped in and seen to it that we are the redeemed of Him.

Ephesians 2:11-13

Therefore, remember that formerly you who are Gentiles by birth and called "uncircumcised" by those who call themselves "the circumcision" (that done in the body by the hands of men) – remember that at that time you were separate from Christ, excluded from citizenship in Israel and foreigners to the covenants of the promise, without hope and without God in the world. But now in Christ Jesus you who once were far away have been brought near through the blood of Christ.

(Related Bible references: Ruth 1:16, 2 Kings 5:15, 1 Chronicles 11:10, Isaiah 2:2-3, Isaiah 65:1, Jeremiah 38:7-13, Jeremiah 48:47, Jeremiah 49:6, Jeremiah 49:39, Daniel 4:34-37, Jonah 1:14-16, Jonah 3:6-10, Malachi 2:13, Acts 15:1-11, Romans 9:4, 1 Corinthians 12:2, Galatians 3:14, Colossians 1:21, James 2:25)

So, why is all this relevant? Why has the Apostle Paul spent almost a chapter and a half telling us so much about the church and its relevance? Why did something on how we are saved get thrown in there? To understand the nature of the church and all who are a part of it, we must also understand what was going on when the Apostle Paul wrote to the Ephesians. The truth is that a lot of the attitudes common in the first century are now common today, in one form or another, especially by those who claim to be people who are all about church. The behaviors are so commonly associated with church, we now call them "church behavior." These typical church behaviors include:

- Angry church mothers and elders who think nothing of mouthing off to anyone in the congregation for any reason.

- Judgmental churchgoers who pick at people's attire, skirt length, the fact that they don't have a hat on, or that they are wearing shorts.

- Preachers who know how to speak-sing, sweat, and theatrically throw themselves all over the altar at just the right time.

- A shift in the beat of the music, letting everyone know when it is time to kick up and start responding to the preacher's words.

- Throwing oil at people, claiming that will deliver them.

- Dramatic altar calls.

- Cueing the church to kick up in the flesh, rather than the Spirit.

While there's nothing wrong with being excited about spiritual things and reflecting that excitement while doing churchy things, the problem with everything I just mentioned is that if we think church is about these things, it proves that we don't have the right attitude and heart that the church should have. There is something wrong with being emotional and dramatic in church to get attention, doing it with the motive to stir up and call attention to the wrong things. Malachi 2:13 says:

Another thing you do: You flood the LORD's altar with tears. You weep and wail because He no longer pays attention to your offerings or accepts them with pleasure from your hands.

This is the very reason why Ephesians 2 is so relevant to us, even today, considering the problems they had in the first century. In this era of church history, Judaism was regarded as an exclusive religion. Due to years of occupation and perversion in the understanding of the law (created by human additions to the law), the Jews believed they were something special of their own merit, and that was separate from truly having right faith in their relationship with God. Being a Jew was based on a national identity, as one that was spiritually and nationally superior to others. They were so exclusive, in fact, that first-century Christians who converted from Judaism didn't understand the process of salvation. They believed it was necessary to become Jewish before one could be a Christian, and that Christians had to uphold the Jewish law to understand Christianity (Acts 15:1-11). This meant human beings made salvation about what race or nation one belonged to rather than the merits of Christ. Enter in the words of salvation, those that remind everyone that salvation is not about what any one of us can do for ourselves. The "uncircumcised" were the nations, who were looked down upon by the Jewish people (the "circumcision") as inferior in every possible way and not able to come to the Father in right relationship, ever.

Even in Old Testament times we see Gentile conversions (Ruth 1:16, 2 Kings 5:15, 1 Chronicles 11:10, Jeremiah 38:7-13, Jonah 1:14-16, Jonah 3:6-10, Daniel 4:34-37, James 2:25). The prophets spoke of a time when the Gentiles would worship alongside the Jews, heralding the praises of the true God (Isaiah 2:2-3). There are words scattered, here and there, that speak of the restoration of surrounding nations into the fold of right standing with God (Jeremiah 48:47, Jeremiah 49:6, 39). The people's ideas were their own creations, a response to a changing world that left them occupied, uncertain, and a minority. The God we meet in the New Testament is the same God of the Old Testament...but the people didn't see it, or perhaps, didn't want to see it. It was more desirable to make spirituality a human product rather than a divine one.

Yet what the apostle teaches us here is very vital

and important in our true understanding of exterior things without internal transformations. Even though the Jews might have had a physical circumcision done by the hands of men, they too were far away from God, because of where their hearts were. Anyone can perform an outward ritual for any reason, but that does not mean that a person is transformed by that ritual. What God has done instead is take those who were far off (Gentiles, nations) – as well as those who were nearer (Jews) – and done something entirely new in them through the work of salvation. It is not something that is done by a cute council or by force, but something done in love, something that brings those who were apart together, into one covenant, one life in Christ Jesus, with one purpose (Galatians 3:14).

Ephesians 2:14-22

For He Himself is our peace, Who has made the two one and has destroyed the barrier, the dividing wall of hostility, by abolishing in His flesh the law with its commandments and regulations. His purpose was to create in Himself one new man out of the two, thus making peace, and in this one body to reconcile both of them to God through the cross, by which He put to death their hostility. He came and preached peace to you who were far away and peace to those who were near. For through Him we both have access to the Father by one Spirit.

Consequently, you are no longer foreigners and aliens, but fellow citizens with God's people and members of God's household, built on the foundation of the apostles and prophets, with Christ Jesus Himself as the chief cornerstone. In Him the whole building is joined together and rises to become a holy temple in the Lord. And in Him, you too are being built together to become a dwelling in which God lives by His Spirit.

(Related Bible references: Psalm 9:11, Psalm 22:28, Psalm 67:2, Psalm 133:1-3, Luke 11:49, John 17:23, Acts 10:35, Romans 2:10, Romans 8:3, Romans 10:12, Romans 11:24, 1 Corinthians 3:10, 1 Corinthians 3:16, 1 Corinthians 6:19, 1 Corinthians 12:13, 1 Corinthians 12:28, Galatians 3:28, Colossians 2:9, Colossians 1:20-22, Colossians 2:14, Colossians 3:11, Hebrews 3:6, Hebrews 7:25, Hebrews 12:2, 1 Peter 2:5, 2 Peter 3:2, Revelation 18:20)

One of the most powerful things that we receive in salvation is peace, but we don't just receive the absence of strife. In Christ, we receive peace as a person, the person of Christ. Christ, in and of Himself, makes us whole. He brings us to a place of wholeness, a place of oneness, where the divisions that create hostilities among communities and within ourselves are no longer present (Psalm 133:1-3). Jesus has made us one in our faith, one with our neighbor in Christ, regardless of where they are from, what they look like, what language they speak, or their income level. He came with peace, heralding it to any who would hear, and from Him, we now all have access to the Father by His one Spirit.

God asks us to come together, to be as one new people, even though we are from all different backgrounds, languages, and cultures. We are a part of this new culture, our Kingdom that is new to us but as old as God's eternal plan, coming together as fellow citizens. God has done a "new" thing within us: it is not a Jewish thing, or a pagan thing, but something else. This is a new thing, marked in Christ, something that no matter how much the world tries to aspire to it with plans that sound good, they will never be able to achieve it. We are not foreign, we are not distant, we are one, in the One Who makes us one, and who turns us around, changing and transforming us into His image.

The church of God is not just spoken of as a body, but also a household, because we know that God is our Father (1 Corinthians 3:10, Hebrews 3:6). We are brothers and sisters in the Lord, one family in many places (Psalm 9:11, Psalm 22:28, Psalm 67:2). That family, in terms of revelation and understanding, is built upon the foundation of the apostles and prophets. This is a fact, found in the Word, that we cannot deny: the Chief Cornerstone (and only chief authority) of the church is Jesus Christ Himself. The foundation that the church is built upon, however, is that of the apostles and prophets.

For the past 200 years or so, much of the church identifies itself as "Evangelical," or trying to create a foundation for the church on the office and work of the evangelist. Once people are evangelized, the "heads" of churches are a combination of bishops and pastors, thus with the church having a uniquely pastoral flair. The problem with this layout is that the church's foundation cannot be built upon an evangelist or a pastor, or anything other than the work of the apostles and prophets. Why is this? The offices of apostle and prophet, which in many ways are designed to function as one, bring the necessary structure and vision to establish the church (Luke 11:49, 1 Corinthians 12:28, 2 Peter 3:2, Revelation 18:20). The prophet carries over from the Old Testament times, bringing discernment and vision to the church, while the apostle, a New Testament office, brings structure, authority, and execution of vision. Both are important and show just how much balance it takes to maintain a spiritual foundation. This also tells us the apostle and prophet still exist today, still with the same purpose, and the same importance, as they did in New Testament times. With the right cornerstone, the right foundation, and those called together worldwide, the church's building is built of its people, worldwide, international, everywhere that they go, as dwellings of the Holy Spirit, the garden, the beauty, the dwelling-place of the Holy Spirit, being built to make sure that God lives and that life shows within each and every one of us, no matter where we are or what we are doing.

It is not lost on us that we are being built, and that our building within Him is progressive (1 Corinthians 3:16, 1 Corinthians 6:19). The body of Christ too builds daily, joins, grows, and becomes more of the image that He desires us to be. We too are being built with the church, as she grows and becomes the impeccable bride, without spot or wrinkle. As we grow in God, we too are transformed, more into the image He desires, with the works He requires, and the life He has given unto us, all within His Spirit.

Chapter Three

The Grace of God in the Apostle and in the Church (Ephesians Chapter 3)

Key verses

- **Verses 2-3:** *Surely you have heard about the administration of God's grace that was given to me for you, that is, the mystery made known to me by revelation, as I have already written briefly.*

- **Verses 5-6:** *...Which was not made known to men in other generations as it has now been revealed by the Spirit to God's holy apostles and prophets. This mystery is that through the Gospel the Gentiles are heirs together with Israel, members together of one body, and sharers together in the promise in Christ Jesus.*

- **Verses 8-9:** *Although I am less than the least of all God's people, this grace was given me: to preach to the Gentiles the unsearchable riches of Christ, and to make plain to everyone the administration of the mystery, which for ages past was kept hidden in God, Who created all things.*

- **Verses 14-15:** *For this reason I kneel before the Father, from Whom His whole family in heaven and on earth derives its name.*

Words and phrases to know

- **Prisoner:** From the Greek word *desmios* which means "bound, in bonds, a captive, a prisoner."[1]

- **Administration:** From the Greek word *oikonomia* which means "the management of a household or of household affairs."[2]

- **Mystery:** From the Greek word *musterion* which means "hidden thing, secret, mystery; of God: the secret counsels which govern God in dealing with the righteous, which are hidden from ungodly and wicked men but plain to the godly; in rabbinic writings, it denotes the mystic or hidden sense: of an OT saying, of an image or form seen in a vision, of a dream."[3]

- **Revelation:** From the Greek word *apokalupsis* which means "a laying bear, making naked; a disclosure of truth, instruction; manifestation, appearance."[4]

- **Generations:** From the Greek word *genea* which means "fathered, birth, nativity; that which has been begotten, men of the same stock, a family; the whole multitude of men living at the same time; an age (i.e. the time ordinarily occupied be each successive generation), a space of 30 - 33 years."[5]

- **Heirs:** From the Greek word *sugkleronomos* which means "a fellow heir, a joint heir; one who obtains something assigned to himself with others, a joint participant."[6]

- **Hidden:** From the Greek word *apokrupto* which means "to hide; concealing, keeping secret."[7]

- **Rulers:** From the Greek word *arche* which means "beginning, origin; the person or thing that commences, the first person or thing in a series, the leader; that by which anything begins to be, the origin, the active cause; the extremity of a thing; the first place, principality, rule, magistracy."[8]

- **Authorities:** From the Greek word *exousia* which means "power of choice, liberty of doing as one pleases; physical and mental power; the power of authority (influence) and of right (privilege); the power of rule or government (the power of him whose will and commands must be submitted to by others and obeyed)."[9]

- **Purpose:** From the Greek word *prothesis* which means "a setting forth of a thing, placing of it in view, the showbread; a purpose."[10]

- **Freedom:** From the Greek word *parrhesia* which means "freedom in speaking, unreservedness in speech; free and fearless confidence, cheerful courage, boldness, assurance; the deportment by which one becomes conspicuous or secures publicity."[11]

- **Confidence:** From the Greek word *pepoithesis* which means "trust, confidence, reliance."[12]

- **Discouraged:** From the Greek word *ekkakeo* which means "to be utterly spiritless, to be wearied out, exhausted."[13]

- **Kneel:** From the Greek word *gonu* which means "the knee, to kneel down."[14]

- **Family:** From the Greek word *patria* which means "lineage running back to some progenitor, ancestry; a race or tribe; family, in a wider sense, nation, people."[15]

- **Strengthen:** From the Greek word *krataioo* which means "to strengthen, make strong; to be made strong, to increase in strength, to grow strong."[16]

- **Immeasurably:** From the Greek word *huper* which means "in behalf of, for the sake of; over, beyond, more than; more, beyond, over."[17]

Ephesians 3:1-6

For this reason I, Paul, the prisoner of Christ Jesus for the sake of you Gentiles – Surely you have heard about the administration of God's grace that was given to me for you, that is, the mystery made known to me by revelation, as I have already written briefly. In reading this, then you will be able to understand my insight into the mystery of Christ, which was not made known to men in other generations as it has now been revealed by the Spirit to God's holy apostles and prophets. This mystery is that through the Gospel the Gentiles are heirs together with Israel, members together of one body, and sharers together in the promise in Christ Jesus.

(Related Bible references: Acts 4:33, Acts 20:28, Romans 11:25, Romans 16:25, 1 Corinthians 15:10, 2 Corinthians 8:1, Colossians 1:24-29, 1 Timothy 3:1, 2 Timothy 4:17)

Most of us know we serve a God Who abounds in grace, but we don't often consider that the grace of God works through the church as much as God's grace reaches out to every one of us as individuals. The church herself is a vessel, a carrier of the grace of God, manifesting it and making it known throughout the world this side of heaven (2 Corinthians 8:1). We can see it visible through the work of salvation, but there are many other ways the work of grace is present within the life of this wonderful gift given to us by God Himself, the church.

It's great to see the grace of God in certain areas, but we can't rightly talk about the church and the grace present in the church without talking about the work of the apostle in the church. The grace of God is present in the church through so many ways, and one of those ways – especially in leadership – is through the ministry and work of the apostle (Acts 4:33, 1 Corinthians 15:10, Colossians 1:24-29, 1 Timothy 3:1). Even though many denominations downplay this aspect of church life and faith, and in particular, try to talk away the office of the apostle, by doing so, they reject one of the prime ways the grace of God flows through the church, blessing both the leaders of the church and the people who are part of it.

In a special way, Ephesians chapter 3 is all about this important discussion, which every church member should study, recognize, and somewhat understand. Here we shall see why we need apostles, why they are relevant, and why they are an important part of the work that God seeks to do within His people, the church.

The Apostle Paul reveals to us a great deal about the apostolic office, especially for modern times, throughout his ministry. Many of his words that we interpret in a general way for leaders were specifically spoken about the apostolic office, and that means we're often missing some of the most insightful perspectives on the apostle because we are trying too hard to interpret the Bible generally. One of the first things that the Apostle Paul clarifies for the Ephesian church in chapter 3 is that there has been a specific administration of God's grace, given to him in his work and his ministry. How does this grace work, and what is it for? The grace of the apostolic office is two-fold:

- **The grace of God works in the apostle, to transform them to do the work that God has appointed them to do:** Being an apostle is something that, while there might be natural qualities within a person that make them a good leader, God does within the person. The amount of responsibility, interest, drive, endurance, and focus needed to lead the church with the vision and purpose of God is something that is beyond personal abilities. It takes grace to be an apostle, it takes grace to do the apostolic work because it is an office of grace, one that extends and shows forth God's love and mercy to leaders, to the church and to the world through the Good News.

- **The grace of God works through the apostle to give a graceful edge to the church:** The world looks at the different movements of God as harsh, punitive or judgmental without considering the entire work of God throughout history. There are long periods where God works quietly, giving people time to repent and turn around. A few incidents by which consequences came around for people's behavior does not make God punitive or harsh. The truth about God's work is that God's entire historical movement has been noted by grace. God always gives people proper time to do what they need to do, He gives space for adjustment and changes, and He, in an all-knowing style, still extends mercy to His people. This grace is present in the apostle, who even though they might desire to do so, doesn't give up on the church. Love the church today or hate the church today, the apostle's foundational work with the church is one God has called them to, and this persistent grace is present in their commitment to see their work with the church through to the very end.

A great summary of the apostolic office and work is found, stated by the Apostle Paul himself, in Colossians 1:24-29:

[Now] I am happy [rejoice] in my sufferings for you. And I accept [fill up; complete] in my body [flesh] what Christ must still suffer [or is lacking in the suffering of Christ] through [or on behalf of] his body, the church. [By suffering while spreading the Gospel, Paul both participates in Christ's death and helps complete God's plan.] I became a servant [minister] of the church because God gave me a special work to do [stewardship; commission] that helps you [for you], and that work is to tell fully [or complete; or preach everywhere; fulfill] the message [word] of God. This message is the secret [mystery; something God had not previously disclosed; Eph. 1:9] that was hidden from everyone since the beginning of time [ages and generations], but now it is made known to God's holy people [the saints]. God decided [chose; willed] to let his people know this rich and glorious secret [mystery; 1:26] which he has for all people [the nations/Gentiles]. This secret [mystery] is that Christ lives in you. He is our only hope for glory [Christ in you, the hope of glory]. So we continue to preach [proclaim; announce] Christ to each person, using all wisdom to warn [instruct; admonish] and to teach everyone, in order to bring each one into God's presence as a mature person in Christ. To do this, I work [toil; labor] and struggle, using Christ's [His] great strength that works so powerfully in me. (EXB)

We have no excuse for misunderstanding the office of the apostle, as there are more examples of the apostle and what they do in the New Testament than any other office. Regardless, it is seriously misunderstood in one form or another. Perhaps it is misunderstood because we don't see enough clear examples of it today, or because those who do claim to embody the office often try so hard to fit in with general church trends that they don't truly walk in its purpose. The apostle isn't more important than the rest of the Ephesians 4:11 ministries, but I do think it's important for us to look at the apostle as its own office. If anyone follows anyone on social media or through the internet who feels they know something about Ephesians 4:11, they often teach that the apostle is "all five of the ministry gifts rolled into one." They believe that being an apostle means being a prophet, a teacher, a pastor, and an evangelist in one big ball. This is a misnomer, because the work of the apostle is an entirely separate work, one that is different from the other four ministry gifts. It is not an all-in-one specialty that is supposed to make the apostolic sound like a mishmash of understanding. The reason people say this, however, is because they don't rightly understand the work of the apostle as its own work, as its own office. Some other myths we hear about the apostolic because we really aren't taking the time to learn about apostles on their own include:

- **The purpose of the apostle is to bring order:** This is a half-truth about apostles, because it is true that in a certain semblance, the apostle does bring a form of order to the church. The problem with the statement is that it is made with the implication that it is the only office of the church that brings order, and that the only point of the apostolic office is to be about a certain sense of order. The truth is that every office of the Ephesians 4:11 ministry brings order to the church and establishes order through their call, each in a different way. So yes, apostles do bring order, but more relevantly, they do so through structure.

- **The apostle is the "thumb" to the Ephesians 4:11 ministry:** I understand the desire to use illustration to teach about the Ephesians 4:11 ministry, believing it makes it easier for people to understand. However, the "hand" imagery in connection with Ephesians 4:11 is causing us more confusion than it is worth. The message given in the teaching is that the thumb's function is more important than that of other fingers, thus that the apostle's office is more important than the rest of the Ephesians 4:11 ministry. The apostolic office isn't more important than other ministers, nor does it have the right to lord authority over other offices.

- **Bishops are the same as apostles:** There is nothing in the New Testament or in the early church writings anywhere that states bishops and apostles are the same office. The bishopric, along with the work of elders and deacons, are a part of the appointments of the church. These works are not necessarily a calling nor a life-long work, but something to which an individual is appointed to, because they desire to be of assistance in the Kingdom (1 Timothy 3:1). Apostles are a part of the Ephesians 4:11 ministry, are duly called to this position, and serve in this calling throughout their lives.

- **Bishops are superior to apostles:** Bishops are a part of the helps ministry of the church. We could call the appointments as the leadership of helps, an essential work that is different from the Ephesians 4:11 ministry. It is not, however, in any way, shape, or form equivalent to the apostolic, or superior to the apostolic. In the New Testament, bishops assisted apostles in their work (Acts 20:28).

- **Apostles are pastors:** In the modern church, we tend to feel out our spiritual leadership understandings through pastors. This means that we associate every single office of the Ephesians

> 4:11 ministry, in one form or another, through the pastoral office. In other words, we think every office looks like, sounds like, and interacts as a pastor. I have met more apostles trying to double as pastors and more pastors trying to double as apostles in the past few years than I have ever in my many years within the faith. Not only is this confusing, it is also misleading. People don't know that an apostle is different from a pastor and respect the differences between the two. This also means a great many of the people who claim to be called to be apostles are, in fact, not, and several who are trying too hard to fit into the pastoral mold are missing their true calling in the apostolic realm.

So, what is the real purpose of the apostolic? I have explained the apostolic in-depth in my book, *Ministry Officer Candidate School* (Righteous Pen Publications, 2026). The view of the apostle in that book is more technical, however, than intimate and relational. Here, the Apostle Paul gives us both an intimate and relational viewpoint of the apostolic, seeing apostles as people, called by God as messengers of His grace. To the Apostle Paul, true apostles everywhere, and anyone who is connected to a true apostle, the apostolic is more than just a role or a work that someone performs. Apostles bring a sense of structure to the church, through their administrative role of establishing, placing, and training leaders. The deeper role of the apostolic, the more intimate portrait which illustrates the apostle's relationship and even struggles with God, is outlined quite well in this chapter: it is to present and reveal the mysteries of Christ. These mysteries, and the understanding of them, come about to the apostle via revelation. The more an apostle learns, the more they are better able to understand and see these important revelations in action, are a foundational aspect to the apostolic office. This makes the work of the apostle a revelatory work, one that brings authority and revelation to the church in a combination that is undeniably important. This tells us what we need to see in a person who claims to be apostolic:

- **Forward moving:** The word "apostle" means "one who is sent." The way this manifests in the apostle is multifold. The apostle is forward thinking, meaning they are often ahead of their time (on average, I have found it to be at least ten years). They can look at a situation and to see the long-term results of it, even if those results are far into the distance. They deal with the constant struggle to get others to see this long-term picture, because many do not see, nor recognize it.

  Apostles are also forward moving in their desire to move forward with the Gospel. They are not content to stay in one place for a long period of time and take an interest in making sure that wherever God assigns them has proper outlets for spiritual growth and development. The apostle doesn't just care about local churches, but about the universal church, including missions, accessibility to spiritual outlets worldwide, training for leaders, spiritual centers, and the spiritual development of the people.

- **Interest in the church:** The work of the apostle builds up the church. Contrary to some popular teachings, the work of the apostle is not to be accomplished in the secular world. The gifts we have as ministers don't flip on and off in our lives, but we don't have them to turn a profit in the business world. It is fine to be an apostle with a secular job or business, but on that secular job or business, the apostle is an individual, not serving as an apostle. The apostolic work is for the church: its growth, its build-up, its function, and its spread.

- **Revelation:** It's fine to cite a reference or be inspired by a book or song, or some other teaching that one receives from time to time. However, if a leader is always getting their teaching and inspiration from someone else, that's a pretty good indication that the person who is delivering the message isn't an apostle. An apostle should be receiving revelation about Scripture from the Word Himself, about matters that pertain to our day and age, about how to make the Bible understandable to people in our times, and about our relationship with God. Apostles should be regularly receiving ideas on how to operate the church better, on how to train leaders in new ways, on how to write or reach out to the world, and on how to better walk in a proper relationship with the church. Apostles are introspective, but only to the point that they receive the needed, necessary teaching to deliver it back to the church.

- **Ability to teach and relay the revelation:** The Apostle Paul specifically states the revelation of these mysteries does not just belong to the apostle, but to the prophet, as well. Where the prophet is more mystical, the apostle is more administrative. Prophetic insights don't always make sense in and of themselves. If anything, they tend to not make much sense to the hearers, especially upon first hearing. They will contain symbols and complex ideas, and sometimes even future events that have yet to manifest. The apostolic work is to not only explain the prophetic, but to understand the things that are not easily understood. They may be things from old, things yet to be, or things generally misunderstood, but it is the work of the apostle to teach and relay that revelation, of which they have divinely inspired understanding.

- **Teaching:** Related to what I just spoke about, apostles aren't just preachers; they are also teachers. They can make things understandable and are able to teach without fanfare, without extreme behavior, and without theatrics. Their word reflects the heart of God, the essential things He desires to speak in this hour, to His people.

- **Discipline:** The structure the apostle brings to the church is in the form of discipline. It is the primary work of the apostle to instruct and work with leaders of the church, helping them to establish the needed leadership, training, and teaching within their churches. The apostle does the work of training and installing those people and then assists those leaders in the oversight of their congregations.

- **Grace-filled:** I have met many leaders who claim to be all about order, but who lack grace. One of the persistent characteristics about the grace of God is its endurance, its long-suffering with us and willingness to work with us, all the way through to the end. If a leader hasn't experienced the grace of God in some way in their life that helps them to extend that grace to others, then that person is either not an apostle or not ready to walk in the office.

The reason the apostle is equipped with this revelation is because the ultimate mystery revealed is the incredible revelation of the church. By the grace of God, all people the world over: Jew and Gentile, woman and man (and everything else in between), and slave and free all have access to be a part of the work of Christ, partaking it within their spiritual lives. It's something the natural mind cannot fathom, but that God reveals by those He calls, and displays His amazing grace to us each time we answer His gentle leading.

Ephesians 3:7-13

I became a servant of this Gospel by the gift of God's grace given me through the working of His power. Although I am less than the least of all God's people, this grace was given me: to preach to the Gentiles the unsearchable riches of Christ, and to make plain to everyone the administration of this mystery, which for ages past was kept hidden in God, Who created all things. His intent was that now, through the church, the manifold wisdom of God should be made known to the rulers and authorities in the heavenly realms, according to His eternal purpose which He accomplished in Christ Jesus our Lord. In Him and through faith in Him we may approach God with freedom and confidence. I ask you, therefore, not to be discouraged because of my sufferings for you, which are your glory.

(Related Bible references: Romans 5:3, Romans 8:18, 1 Corinthians 2:7, 1 Corinthians 15:9, 2 Corinthians 5:11-21, Galatians 1:16, Colossians 1:16-18, Colossians 1:27, 1 Timothy 1:14, 2 Timothy 2:10, Hebrews 1:2, Hebrews 4:15-16, 1 Peter 3:14, 1 Peter 3:22)

The basic principle of every apostolic ministry should be this powerful ministry of reconciliation made real and living through the work of grace. Received in humility, recognizing the position of the apostle as one of importance, but the apostle not viewing themselves as personally important, the apostolic work goes forth by God's power, and nothing else. It is the apostle's job to preach to the nations, beyond what is immediate or comfortable, beyond what is seen, into the unseen. The apostle knows, by revelation, this mystery which must be revealed with freedom and confidence. Therefore, the apostolic office is not one to be ashamed of, nor is it one to ignore. It is an unveiling, bringing forth explanation of every type and shadow we can find, that will be made known to all who are both high and low in this world (2 Corinthians 5:11-21).

Thanks to Christ, we can approach God with freedom and confidence. We can go boldly before the throne (Hebrews 4:16) to obtain mercy and find His grace, as we go with our present state of humility within us. We know who we are, and we know Who God is, and the magnitude of all that He does for us. We are neither distant to God, nor indifferent to Him. He knows our every move, our every heart, and our every petition before Him.

For our High Priest is able [For we do not have a high priest who is unable] to understand [sympathize with] our weaknesses. He was tempted in every way that we are, but He did not sin. (Hebrews 4:15, EXB)

Do we consider the depth of what it means to have a "high priest who understands" and what a movement of grace that is in and of itself? In many churches, it's obvious the leaders do not understand what the people they lead go through or encounter. They are met with harsh responses and with unkind sentiments. The sting of judgment is felt going out and coming in. We have come to associate that sort of stigma, that sting, that bitterness we feel from our leaders with the work of Jesus Christ. Let's never forget that Jesus died for our sins, fully willing to lay down His life for every one of us. Before His death, Jesus became man and walked among us, experiencing the pains, suffering, and difficulties of human life. He experienced that as a high priest Who understands: He knows our temptations, our faults, our feelings, our difficulties, our pains and our weaknesses, and still invites us to come forward in freedom, in grace, in love, with everything we speak, need, and think.

Therefore, never be discouraged by the sufferings

that people of faith go through, no matter how difficult they might be. The sufferings that true leaders encounter (and true believers, as well) are not because they are bad, have deep, hidden sins, or don't have enough faith. Things happen; we live in a hostile world that doesn't always respond to us very well, and we don't always respond well to it. We stand, however, as people who are fully well invested in this work, and we know that Jesus is with us, understanding, guiding, supporting, and lifting us, no matter what it is that we encounter for Him this side of heaven. He picks us up when we fall, protects us from that which is seen and unseen, and that which causes us to change as much as that which causes us to hold fast (Romans 5:3, Romans 8:18, 1 Peter 3:14).

Ephesians 3:14-21

For this reason I kneel before the Father, from Whom His whole family in heaven and on earth derives its name. I pray that out of His glorious riches He may strengthen you with power through His Spirit in your inner being, so that Christ may dwell in your hearts through faith. And I pray that you, being rooted and established in love, may have power, together with all the saints, to grasp how wide and long and high and deep is the love of Christ, and to know this love that surpasses knowledge – that you may be filled to the measure of all the fullness of God.

Now to Him Who is able to do immeasurably more than all we ask or imagine, according to His power that is at work within us, to Him be glory in the church and in Christ Jesus throughout all generations, forever and ever! Amen.

(Related Bible references: Psalm 95:6, Matthew 19:26, Mark 10:27, John 1:16, Acts 20:36, Romans 11:33, 1 Corinthians 2:9, Philippians 4:9, Colossians 1:23, Colossians 2:9, Hebrews 13:21)

Because of the grace that the Apostle Paul received, experienced, and extended to others, he knew that he could kneel before his Maker without any question to intercede on behalf of the church (Psalm 95:6). The church was a part of him, and he was a part of the church. Inseparable, one, continuing between heaven and earth, the family of God derives its identity from God, its positioning from God, its purpose from God. The Apostle Paul knew he could pray for His glorious riches to overtake the church, so the Gospel could continue into all the world. He knew how important it was for Christ to dwell within us, for the Spirit of God to permeate us into far beyond mere words into deep fruitage that changes our lives, and that our faith might change who we are. He knew we needed to be rooted and established in love, because love is the source of our power, our transformation, and our true establishment.

It is only when we are rooted in love that we can even begin to fathom the love of Christ, which we will never understand by our mere logic or even fully with our faith, this side of heaven. It surpasses all knowledge, all our ideas, and everything with it – but we are to be filled with every measure of it, which is God's love. If we will only allow ourselves to be full of His love, we will experience that flood of completion in our own lives that brings meaning to each task.

God can do all things, beyond anything we can think of, imagine, or perceive (Matthew 19:26, Mark 10:27). We give Him all the glory and honor: in the church, in the world, in our homes, and among our communities, perpetually for all generations. Eternity is not enough time to sing how great is our God and herald His marvelous works to any who have ears to hear. Certainly, we love our God, we praise Him, we bless His Name, and we rejoice that He has given us this wonderful Kingdom with grace-filled leadership to be a part of: His Church.

Chapter Four

THE BELIEF, LEADERSHIP, AND LIFE OF THE CHURCH (EPHESIANS CHAPTER 4)

Key verses

- **Verse 1:** *As a prisoner for the Lord, then, I urge you to live a life worthy of the calling you have received.*

- **Verses 4-5:** *There is one body and one Spirit – just as you were called to one hope when you were called – one Lord, one faith, one baptism; one God and Father of all, Who is over all and through all and in all.*

- **Verses 11-12:** *It was He Who gave some to be apostles, some to be prophets, some to be evangelists, and some to be pastors and teachers, to prepare God's people for works of service, so that the body of Christ may be built up.*

- **Verse 16:** *From Him the whole body, joined and held together by every supporting ligament, grows and builds itself up in love, as each part does its work.*

- **Verses 25-27:** *Therefore each of you must put off falsehood and speak truthfully to his neighbor, for* *we are all members of one body. "In your anger do not sin": Do not let the sun go down while you are still angry, and do not give the devil a foothold.*

- **Verse 32:** *Be kind and compassionate to one another, forgiving each other, just as in Christ God forgave you.*

Words and phrases to know

- **Worthy:** From the Greek word *axios* which means "suitably, worthily, in a manner worthy of."[1]
- **Humble:** From the Greek word *tapeinophrosune* which means "the having a humble opinion of one's self; a deep sense of one's (moral) littleness; modesty, humility, lowliness of mind."[2]
- **Gentle:** From the Greek word *praotes* which means "gentleness, mildness, meekness."[3]
- **Patience:** From the Greek word *makrothumia* which means "patience, endurance, constancy, steadfastness, perseverance; patience, forbearance, longsuffering, slowness in avenging wrongs."[4]
- **Unity:** From the Greek word *henotes* which means "unity; unanimity, agreement."[5]
- **One:** From the Greek word *heis* which means "one."[6]
- **Called:** From the Greek word *klesis* which means "a calling, calling to; a call, invitation."[7]
- **Baptism:** From the Greek word *baptisma* which means "immersion, submersion."[8]

- **Gifts:** From the Greek word *doma* which means "a gift."[9]

- **Apostles:** From the Greek word *apostolos* which means "a delegate, messenger, one sent forth with orders."[10]

- **Prophets:** From the Greek word *prophetes* which means "in Greek writings, an interpreter of oracles or of other hidden things; one who, moved by the Spirit of God and hence his organ or spokesman, solemnly declares to men what he has received by inspiration, especially concerning future events, and in particular such as relate to the cause and kingdom of God and to human salvation; a poet (because poets were believed to sing under divine inspiration)."[11]

- **Evangelists:** From the Greek word *euaggelistes* which means "a bringer of good tidings, an evangelist; the name given to the NT heralds of salvation through Christ who are not apostles."[12]

- **Pastors:** From the Greek word *poimen* which means "a herdsman, esp. a shepherd; metaph. the manager, director, of any assembly, of the overseers of the Christian assemblies."[13]

- **Teachers:** From the Greek word *didaskalos* which means "a teacher; in the NT one who teaches concerning the things of God, and the duties of man."[14]

- **Service:** From the Greek word *diakonia* which means "service, ministering, esp. of those who execute the commands of others; of those who by the command of God proclaim and promote religion among men; the ministration of those who render to others the offices of Christian affection esp. those who help meet need by either collecting or distributing of charities; the office of the deacon in the church; the service of those who prepare and present food."[15]

- **Mature:** From the Greek word *teleios* which means "brought to its end, finished; wanting nothing necessary to completeness; perfect; that which is perfect."[16]

- **Infants:** From the Greek word *nepios* which means "an infant, little child; a minor, not of age; metaph. childish, untaught, unskilled."[17]

- **Tossed back and forth:** From the Greek word *kludonizomai* which means "to be tossed by waves."[18]

- **Cunning:** From the Greek word *kubeia* which means "dice playing; metaph. the deception of men, because dice players sometimes cheated and defrauded their fellow players."[19]

- **Craftiness:** From the Greek word *panourgia* which means "cleverness, craftiness."[20]

- **Deceitful scheming:** From the Greek word *plane* which means "a wandering, a straying about; metaph. mental straying, error which shows itself in action, a wrong mode of acting, error, that which leads into error, deceit or fraud."[21]

- **Grow up:** From the Greek word *auxano* which means "to cause to grow, augment; to increase, become greater; to grow, increase."[22]

- **Head:** From the Greek word *kephale* which means "the head, both of men and often of animals. Since the loss of the head destroys life, this word is used in the phrases relating to capital and extreme punishment; prominent."[23]

- **Ligament:** From the Greek word *haphe* which means "bond, connection."[24]

- **Falsehood:** From the Greek word *pseudos* which means "a lie; conscious and intentional falsehood; in a broad sense, whatever is not what it seems to be."[25]

- **Truthfully:** From the Greek word *aletheia* which means "objectively what is true in any matter under consideration, what is true in things appertaining to God and the duties of man, moral and religious truth, the truth as taught in the Christian religion, respecting God and the execution of his purposes through Christ, and respecting the duties of man, opposing alike to the superstitions of the Gentiles and the inventions of the Jews, and the corrupt opinions and precepts of false teachers even among Christians; subjectively truth as a personal excellence."[26]

- **Neighbor:** From the Greek word *plesion* which means "a neighbour."[27]

- **Anger:** From the Greek word *orgizo* which means "to provoke, to arouse to anger; to be provoked to anger, be angry, be wroth."[28]

- **Foothold:** From the Greek word *topos* which means "place, any portion or space marked off, as it were from surrounding space; metaph. the condition or station held by one in any company or assembly, opportunity, power, occasion for acting."[29]

- **Stealing:** From the Greek word *klepto* which means "to steal."[30]

- **Unwholesome talk:** From two Greek words: *sapros* which means "rotten, putrefied; corrupted by one and no longer fit for use, worn out; of poor quality, bad, unfit for use, worthless,"[31] and *logos* which means "of speech, a word, uttered by a living voice, embodies a conception or idea, what someone has said, discourse, doctrine, teaching, anything reported in speech; a narration, narrative, matter under discussion, thing spoken of, affair, a matter in dispute, case, suit at law, the thing spoken of or talked about; event, deed; its use as respect to the MIND alone, reason, the mental faculty of thinking, meditating, reasoning, calculating, account, i.e. regard, consideration, account, i.e. reckoning, score, account, i.e. answer or explanation in reference to judgment, relation, i.e. with whom as judge we stand in relation; In John, denotes the essential Word of God, Jesus Christ, the personal wisdom and power in union with God, his minister in creation and government of the universe, the cause of all the world's life both physical and ethical, which for the procurement of man's salvation put on human nature in the person of Jesus the Messiah, the second person in the Godhead, and shone forth conspicuously from His words and deeds."[32]

- **Grieve:** From the Greek word *lupeo* which means "to make sorrowful; to affect with sadness, cause grief, to throw into sorrow; to grieve, offend; to make one uneasy, cause him a scruple."[33]

- **Sealed:** From the Greek word *sphragizo* which means "to set a seal upon, mark with a seal, to seal."[34]

- **Bitterness:** From the Greek word *pikria* which means "bitter gall."[35]

- **Rage:** From the Greek word *thumos* which means "passion, angry, heat, anger forthwith boiling up and soon subsiding again; glow, ardour, the wine of passion, inflaming wine (which either drives the drinker mad or kills him with its strength)."[36]

- **Brawling:** From the Greek word *kakia* which means "malignity, malice, ill-will, desire to injure; wickedness, depravity; evil, trouble."[37]

- **Slander:** From the Greek word *blasphemia* which means "slander, detraction, speech injurious, to another's good name; impious and reproachful speech injurious to divine majesty."[38]

- **Compassionate:** From the Greek word *eusplagchnos* which means "having strong bowels; compassionate, tender hearted."[39]

Ephesians 4:1-6

As a prisoner for the Lord, then, I urge you to live a life worthy of the calling you have received. Be completely humble and gentle; be patient, bearing with one another in love. Make every effort to keep the unity of the Spirit through the bond of peace. There is one body and one Spirit – just as you were called to one hope when you were called – one Lord, one faith, one baptism, one God and Father or all, Who is over all and through all and in all.

(Related Bible references: Numbers 6:26, Proverbs 12:20, Psalm

133:1-3, Isaiah 11:2, Haggai 2:9, John 17:23, Acts 20:19, Acts 27:1, Romans 6:3, Romans 12:3-5, Romans 16:4-6, 1 Corinthians 1:10-17, 1 Corinthians 6:17, 1 Corinthians 8:6, 1 Corinthians 12:13, 1 Corinthians 13:4, 1 Corinthians 16:19, 2 Corinthians 4:1-10, 2 Corinthians 5:8, 2 Corinthians 8:18, Philippians 1:27, Philippians 2:3, Colossians 3:15, Colossians 4:10, 1 Timothy 3:15, 2 Timothy 1:8, Philemon 1:1, Hebrews 12:1-3, 1 Peter 3:11, 1 Peter 5:5)

The book of Ephesians has, thus far, shown us the church's existence for all time, who is in the church, and the work of grace present in the ministry of the apostle. The uniquely spiritual components and insights present within Ephesians up to this point prepare us for more of the practical aspects, which Ephesians deals with in its remaining three chapters. The reason for this is simple: we often make the statement, "First the natural, then the spiritual." The statement itself is from 1 Corinthians 15:46 and speaks of the resurrection; that first we have natural bodies, and then we will, at the resurrection, experience spiritual transformation of our physical being. It doesn't, however, refer to the long-term plan of God in the church, as we can see here in Ephesians. Ephesians points out that anything going on in the natural realm has already been foreseen and planned for in the spiritual realm. Everything we see here, God foreknew. He has always had a plan and a response to those things that we see. His response, in fact, to many of the complaints we see in this world today is, indeed, the church, and the church's proper positioning for what He has ordained it to do. If the church would accept its purpose in God's plan and stop trying to court the world while being married to the Savior, the answers that we seek would be met through God's church. The church was never created to be trendy, emerging, happening, or seeker-oriented, but to be eternally current while being spiritually relevant. The more we realize this, the more we will realize that the call to step up is ours. We are waiting on God to do something He has already done; it's us that refuse to move forward.

Seeing the spiritual first, the book of Ephesians takes on a very practical, everyday tone in its advice, its advisements, and its perspective. We understand that the church is a spiritual Kingdom, something that reflects spiritual values, and is valuable beyond what we can just see. The church is more than the people that belong to it this side of heaven. The church is more than just how one person in it may act, feel, behave, or think. This eternal truth is important for us to keep in mind, especially when we consider how many different opinions, feelings, thoughts, and approaches people must matters of faith.

God knew, in His infinite plan, that people of all different cultures, nations, and backgrounds would not see everything exactly the same when it came to things of faith. We have many different denominations and denominational perspectives because people don't all read everything in the Bible in the same way, and there are some matters that we can see differently without jeopardizing our salvation. We should never mistake this needed balance as an excuse to believe whatever we want, have whatever leadership we want in church, or do whatever we want. Ephesians 4 addresses our needed essentials for the practical side of faith: what we need to believe, what leaders we need, and how we need to live.

The Apostle Paul was a prisoner for the Lord in more than one way, thus making this statement a double entendre of sorts. Yes, he was literally a prisoner, imprisoned for his faith, at the time of this letter (Acts 27:1, Colossians 4:10, 2 Timothy 1:8, Philemon 1:1). The Apostle Paul was bound for the Lord in a deeper way, however, than just by the mere politics of his era. The Apostle Paul was also a prisoner for the Lord, in the sense that his commitment to God was a life-long service and something he was bound to, day in and day out, from the point of his conversion throughout the rest of his life. Being an apostle and doing the work of the

Lord was not a simple task, not by a longshot. Sometimes doing it must have seemed like, as we would call it, a "life sentence." This doesn't diminish the relevance of his work, however. It was his connection to his call that allowed the Apostle Paul to urge, indicating an immediate need for such in the church, that those who would be a part of the church would live their lives worthy of the calling that they received. What does this mean? It means that the Apostle Paul desired the church to become "saved all the way," as some might say. He wanted to see people live in accordance with the calling, allowing the two perspectives to become one. Too often we want to have our faith life (our calling life) and our secular life, and neither one touches the other. God knew that the concept of sacred and secular in one being doesn't work that simply and thus didn't create us to be so dichotomous. It doesn't work like this, because our faith is to be a part of our lives as many threads are woven together to form a single fabric. We can't pull out one thread of a fabric and still have the fabric remain the same. So too it should be with our faith. Our calling, both to salvation and to whatever it is that God has called us to do in this life, should be interwoven into who we are. It should transform the aspects of our lives that need transformation and enhance those aspects of our lives that are on the right track.

Our callings from God should not puff us up, causing us to become arrogant. Whether we are called to leadership in the church, work in the business world, private enterprise, agriculture, single life, home life, or any other option for life skills and work, what we do, if we are in God's will, is a calling. It is He Who gives us the ability to do it, and not us, ourselves. It is the same parallel as salvation being from Him, and not of us (2 Corinthians 4:1-10). We are not just called to do a work, but to be a spiritual people, walking in His grace. The ancient world did not see a difference between someone's work and their faith, and as a result, many things frequently overlapped in the pagan culture of the day. The best way for us to display the worthiness of our calling is to be humble, gentle, and patient, bearing with one another in love. This means we don't esteem ourselves too highly, we consider how we treat other people, we are not haughty or placing ourselves above others in the form of impatience, and we know how to bear with one another: we do so with grace, extending the love of God to other people. It also means, on the inverse, that we don't provoke others with our negative behavior.

The unity of the Spirit is something we tapped into a bit in chapter 2, but the Apostle Paul expounds it here, in a different way. More than something that should just be a nice ideal for the church to aspire to, it is something that is absolutely essential, a requirement of belief and doctrinal understanding. Whenever anyone brings up the topic of unity in church, people all get warm and fuzzy and start nodding their heads in agreement. Most Christians I have met universally agree there is a general unity disconnect in church today. They will stop and say how churches shouldn't be noted by denominations and should work together to accomplish more projects, but it typically ends there. This type of thinking is part of why we have a unity problem within the church. Unity is more than a council that gets together to accomplish a project and talk about how the church should be more unified. It's not the concept of a body politic, which creates more of a question as to who should be in charge or what we should be doing. The way we often approach unity in the church is perhaps the clearest example that we don't have the first clue as to what unity truly is and how it can change our understanding of the church.

The church is severely disconnected in modern times, no question. I don't deny that we are divided over things that are often not truly important in the perspectives of eternity and that we are busy operating the church out of vanity and conceit, rather than spiritual principle. The unity we need to look at, however, is not the unity that we often discuss. The Scriptures teach us that the bond of unity comes through the work of the Spirit. We can't do unity on our own, no matter how much we might try. It takes a work of the Spirit within each person as well as within the general interworking of a ministry or church to find the point of unity that not only brings us together, but keeps us together. If we are to be united in the Spirit, then that means there are five different levels of unity that the church should operate in, for it to accomplish God's purposes for it:

- **Unity with God:** We can't be united as a church if we are not united with God. Union with God is a spiritual precept, something that is often expressed in the Scriptures as the church being married to God in one form or another. We are going to look at this aspect of our faith more in chapter 5, but I will speak on it briefly here. The purpose of the church is not to be united to any worldly ideal or common goal above that of being united with God. Our churches should never be about national, political, social, or goal-oriented ideals, because this distracts us from our relationship with God. Our earthly connections and aspirations to one another should not be the focus of the church, the Bride of Christ.

  We can also be united to certain people or ideals in church more than we are united to God. If we are united to our leader more than we are united to God, if we are in church because we are looking for a spouse or for human companionship, or if we are interested in church for social, political, or career ambitions, we are in church for the wrong reason. Our purpose in church, going to church, and being the church is because we recognize the power of becoming one with God, as He has saved us and invited us to enter eternal life with Him (1 Corinthians 6:17).

- **Unity with one another:** Faith is not just about us or how we feel about God. Our unity as family in Christ comes because we are first in Christ, and being in Christ means we are a part of the church. It does matter how we treat one another, and it does matter how we interact with one another. Just like in natural families, being a part of the church means learning how to get along, how to work with one another, how to handle those we do not like, and how to work together for the cause of the Gospel. God expects us to learn how to put aside our differences and come together for eternity, because that is exactly how long we will all spend our lives together (Psalm 133:1-3).

- **Unity with the universal church:** The church should never consider itself to just be one local entity. It's great to belong to a local church; it is even necessary for the spiritual life and growth of an individual. If we get too caught up in the local church mentality, however, we will lose sight of the fact that the church does not just consist of a local church. The local church is an extension of the universal church, and a part of the universal church. We should never forget the Gospel's message is destined to travel the world over, and that there are believers and laborers working worldwide to ensure the message gets to every creature, just as it should (Romans 16:4-6, 1 Corinthians 16:19, 1 Timothy 3:15).

- **Unity with other churches and ministries:** Akin to being a part of the universal church is being in union with other churches. Historically speaking, church associations and denominations used to have annual conventions or convocations or what was coined as "fifth Sunday fellowships" so many times per year. These events helped to remind churchgoers that their church experience was bigger than they were, and it was bigger than they were in an immediate sense, one they could see with their own eyes. Whether it is feeling the need to prove something by working with a different Christian denomination or it is accomplished by seeing the different way that churches are connected within a singular association or group, churches should assemble for events, different projects, support for what other churches are doing, and for those who are in itinerant ministry or missions (1 Corinthians 16:19, 2 Corinthians 8:18).

- **Unity with history:** The church of the ages that is no longer here on earth is present with the Lord (2 Corinthians 5:8). They are a part of eternity, even though they are no longer in their bodies. They worship the Lord at the seat of His throne, giving glory to Him day and night, in His presence, serving Him. As Christians, we should recognize that we did not get here by ourselves, and that the road of Christian martyrdom, doctrinal foundations, leadership, and purpose have all been long preserved by individuals who are no longer with us on earth. The Kingdom of God is bigger than just what is laid out here on earth, and we should take note to make sure we do not miss it because our experience with church has only gone on for a period during our earthly existence (Hebrews 12:1-3).

These five points of unity means that there is a long disconnect in modern churches between the universal church, the unity of church history, internal unity within churches, communication with other churches, and in some instances, even our own unity with God. If we have the chronic issue of not being able to discern who is a true part of the church from who is not and we either constantly disconnect or constantly connect ourselves to demons or the doctrine of demons, we don't understand just how important unity is, or what it means to us (John 17:23).

Unity is expressed through the bond of peace (Numbers 6:26, Proverbs 12:20, Haggai 2:9, 1 Peter 3:11). This tells us that peace is a bond, an assurance, something that keeps the church together, meaning that, for the most part, the church should reflect a peaceful state of wholeness, where each member is at some semblance of peace with one another. I don't think we realize just how much it takes to accomplish this, especially in a world of vexing and contrary church folk. We can't have a fighting, quarreling church because then it's not in the bond of peace, and it is not abiding by its own beliefs. If we believe God can make us whole and make us one with Him, then we can believe that He can do that with the entire church. It doesn't mean that we are one in a worldly sense, united by some sort of political identity, singular leader, or empowered cause (save that of the Gospel). It does mean that the internal strife that often plagues churches can cease, in favor of the bigger spiritual picture that we are called to embrace.

The Apostle Paul goes on to outline the essence of the oneness of the church, rather than the pluralities that we often think of when we think of church. He does this by emphasizing that there are seven common elements, regardless of peripherals, that mark the church as one, because recognizing these things as one sets the church apart as unique among other religions. In a polytheistic world that believed in a plurality of gods and deities, the church contrasted such by saying that there were not many, but only one:

- **One body:** The church. No matter how many local churches may exist in a city or in different cities, there is only one body of Christ, and that is the church.

- **One Spirit:** The Holy Spirit, sometimes called the "sevenfold Spirit" because it is noted for bringing seven attributes (as found in Isaiah 11:2: wisdom, understanding, guidance, power, knowledge, respect of the Lord, right judgment), seven being the number which represents perfection and the perfection of God. No matter how many spiritual gifts we recognize or how many are touched by the Spirit, there is only one Spirit.

- **One hope to which we are called:** The hope to which we are called is heavenward, but not in a sense of death. It is in the sense of the fact that our Lord and our Father is in heaven, and that the hope of salvation comes from the Father and the Son. Our hope, for everything in this world, natural or spiritual, lies in the Lord.

- **One Lord:** Our Lord is Jesus Christ. We do not serve many lords, but one singular Lord. Jesus was not replaced with an emperor or successor when He died. He rose again, and is still our one Lord, even though He is now ascended to heaven.

- **One faith:** There is only one faith, not multiple faiths. While we may all each individually believe in God and have different ways that we express what we have experienced with God, there is only one, saving faith that leads us to eternal life with God.

- **One baptism:** Baptismal immersions were common in ancient times, as they signified the school of thought that one followed theologically or philosophically. They were a mark of what one had been taught, and the individual was immersed in the name of the teacher that taught that student, signifying they were immersed in that way of thinking. It is for this reason that baptism was often a particularly decisive point of contention in the early church:

I beg [urge; appeal to] you, brothers and sisters, by the Name [or by the authority; or as followers] of our Lord Jesus Christ that all of you agree with each other and not be split into groups [divided into factions]. I beg that you be completely joined together [fully united; or made complete] by having the same kind of thinking [mind] and the same purpose [intention; conviction]. My brothers and sisters, some people from Chloe's family [household; these could be family members, servants, or business agents] have told me quite plainly [reported to me] that there are quarrels [conflicts; rivalries] among you. This is what I mean: One of you says, "I follow Paul"; another says, "I follow Apollos"; another says, "I follow Peter [Cephas; Peter's name in Aramaic; 3:22; 9:5; 15:5; Mark 1:30; John 1:42]"; and another says, "I follow Christ." Christ has been divided up into different groups! [or Is Christ divided?] Did Paul die on the cross for you? No! Were you baptized in the name of Paul? No! ["No!" is implied but not stated in the Greek.] I thank God I did not baptize any of you except Crispus and Gaius so that now no one can say you were baptized in my name. (I also baptized the family [household] of Stephanas, but I do not remember if I baptized anyone else.) [For] Christ did not send me to baptize people but to preach the Good News [Gospel], and not using words of human wisdom [or eloquent language; clever speech] so that the cross of Christ [the message of Christ's sacrificial death on the cross] would not lose its power [or become meaningless; be emptied]. (1 Corinthians 1:10-17, EXB)

The Apostle Paul reminds us here that there is only one baptism and not many, and that baptism is not into the teachers that we follow or the teachers that we personally love, even though God has sent them into our lives for our edification and education. We are baptized into Jesus Christ; not just into His teaching, but into His death, that we might rise again in resurrection:

Did you forget [or Don't you know] that all of us who became part of Christ Jesus when we were baptized [were baptized into Christ Jesus] shared His death in that baptism [or participated in His death through that baptism; were baptized into His death]. (Romans 6:3, EXB)

Our baptism experience signifies something different than just merely being saturated with a teaching or a doctrinal system. They signify that we have become one with Christ, we have died with Him in His death, and that when we come up out of the waters of baptism, we have been raised to new life. In our resurrection, we are part of His Body, the church. There is only one baptism that can accomplish this, and it is baptism into Christ.

- **One God and Father of all:** There is only one God, our Father, not multiple gods, who demand various things from each of us. God is one, and God will remain one, no matter how many Christians there will be throughout the ages.

In summary, the one God and Father of all is over all, through all, and all in all. He is the reason behind creation, the reason behind salvation, the reason behind the church, the reason why each and every one of us is able to call ourselves a part of the church, is the giver of all our spiritual gifts and abilities, and is the driving force behind all that we, as people who claim to be a part of the church, should recognize.

Ephesians 4:7-16

But to each one of us grace has been given as Christ apportioned it. This is why it says:

***"When He ascended on high,
He led captives in His train
and gave gifts to men."***

(What does "He ascended" mean except that He also descended to the lower, earthly regions? He Who descended is the very One Who ascended higher than all the heavens, in order to fill the whole universe.) It was He Who gave some to be apostles, some to be prophets, some to be evangelists, and some to be pastors and teachers, to prepare God's people for works of service, so that the body of Christ may be built up until we all reach unity in the faith and in the knowledge of the Son of God and become mature, attaining to the whole measure of the fullness of Christ.

Then we will no longer be infants, tossed back and forth by the waves, and blown here and there by every wind of teaching and by the cunning and craftiness of men in their deceitful scheming. Instead, speaking the truth in love, we will in all things grow up into Him Who is the Head, that is, Christ. From Him the whole body, joined and held together by every supporting ligament, grows and builds itself up in love, as each part does its work.

(Related Bible references: Deuteronomy 4:1-10, 1 Samuel 19:18-24, Psalm 23:1-6, Psalm 68:18, Isaiah 30:20-21, Isaiah 61:1-3, Jeremiah 3:15-16, Jeremiah 12:10-17, Ezekiel 2:1-10, Hosea

12:10, Amos 3:7, Matthew 10:2, Matthew 10:41, Matthew 12:38, Matthew 13:57, Luke 4:14-21, John 10:11-14, Acts 2:42, Acts 8:5-6, Acts 8:27-40, Acts 13:1, Acts 21:8, 1 Corinthians 4:1-2, 1 Corinthians 4:17, 1 Corinthians 12:11, 1 Corinthians 12:27-31, 1 Corinthians 14:31-32, 1 Corinthians 14:36-40, Ephesians 2:19-21, Ephesians 3:5, Philippians 2:22, Colossians 1:28, 1 Timothy 1:18, 1 Timothy 3:16, 1 Timothy 4:1-9, 1 Timothy 5:22, 2 Timothy 1:6, 2 Timothy 2:22, 2 Timothy 4:5, Titus 2:4-7, Hebrews 3:1, Hebrews 6:2, Hebrews 9:24, Hebrews 13:9, James 1:4, James 3:13-14, 2 Peter 1:12-21, 2 Peter, 1 John 3:18, 1 John 4:1-3, 2:1-22, Revelation 1:4, Revelation 10:9-11)

Ephesians 4 now passes from the things we must believe as a church in a doctrinal sense to the essential leadership God has given to us in order to see to it that the church functions properly, as one body. It makes perfect sense that once the essentials of belief are sorted out, that the church can think of other more practical matters that relate to church life. The next logical area of examination is that of leadership, or the way that the church will operate.

Many think church leadership is unfair, showing God as partial, rather than treating all believers the same. The idea that God calls certain individuals to lead and not others sounds like a reason for modern churchgoers to protest, citing such is unfair and somehow wrong of God. Most who espouse this viewpoint take grave issue with attending church and often come up against leaders who are in positions of authority in the worst way.

This is a very immature view of leadership and a very immature concept of the ways of God and of the gifts of God. God is not partial, by any stretch of the imagination, but it also does not mean that our interaction, experience, or calling from God is exactly the same. This is different from being partial. It recognizes that people are different, given different abilities, and that God expects us all to use the abilities He has given us, for His glory. In the natural, we all recognize that we aren't all good at the same things and we don't all have the same abilities. We can understand

and see that some people are natural leaders, while other people are more inclined to be followers. The same is true from a spiritual perspective. Some people are called to be leaders and are gifted to be such because God recognizes the abilities to do so within them. Other people are called to be a part of the church and to participate in the church, walking in the gifts that the Spirit has given to them, and building up the church in the form of everyday life and living.

The realities of church leadership are that they require a special form of grace and that they require a great amount of responsibility and tasks that most people are not called to handle. It doesn't mean that leaders are better or more important in the church than anyone else, it just means that the way they are called to work in and through church is different than those who are not called to leadership. It's about more than just being issued papers and ordained by a human being; it is about being a part of the order and ministry of God. It also means that being genuinely called to ministry is not nearly as common as it looks to many today. I have theorized what I call the "thirds rule," which establishes that the church consists of approximately one-third leadership and two-thirds laity. A good portion of those called to leadership (two of the five offices) will often be working to establish new congregations or in ministries that take them beyond the local church, meaning that several will not be consistently seen in the same church every week. No one's local congregation should consist of all ministers, nor should all churches exist to specialize in leadership development (because this means a church is full of leaders and focusing on leaders rather than balancing the church for optimal Kingdom growth and expansion). As a result, it is important for us to consider just what Kingdom leadership is designed to look like, and what model we should follow when considering who to join with in church membership.

It is unrealistic to think God has set the church

without proper leadership, and even more unrealistic to think that the leadership pattern He has established for the church is foreign, confusing, hard to figure out, or different from what it was in first century times. God has seen to it that each one of us – every member of the church – has been given a certain level of grace, because in the work of Christ, He did not only apportion to us salvation, but also certain gifts. These gifts are the work of grace in our lives, things that we cannot work within ourselves, but that God has given to us, for the betterment of the church.

While God has appointed grace to all, some of the gifts that God has given by grace are specifically for leadership. It is important we pay attention to the word "some," because it means that not everyone is given these gifts. These gifts, the teaching gifts for the church, are also those called to church leadership. These gifts are:

- Apostle
- Prophet
- Evangelist
- Pastor
- Teacher

Even though the work of each aspect of the Ephesians 4:11 ministry is a little different, there are certain things we can see about the five-fold as we look at the Scriptures, which pertain to all aspects of it:

- **A gift:** The Ephesians 4:11 ministry are gifts both to the individual minister who is endowed by God to walk in their office, while they are also a gift to the entire body of Christ. The Ephesians 4:11 ministry is given to the church freely, purposed to equip the work of the church, and to help us develop into the stature and work of Christ. To reject the Ephesians 4:11 ministry gifts is to reject God, as He is the One Who gave these gifts to us.

- **A calling:** Each aspect of the Ephesians 4:11 ministry is a calling, meaning that God has called those in the Ephesians 4:11 ministry (who rightly hold their positions) to their work. It is not something they were appointed to do, and it may very well not be something they desire. They are equipped, by God's grace, to complete and fulfill that calling, which they answer in Christ. It cannot be turned on and off at whim, and when one desires to be intimately acquainted with a member of the Ephesians 4:11 ministry, they must be prepared for the unique way that individual will answer their call.

- **An office:** To describe the positions of apostle, prophet, evangelist, pastor and teacher as "an office" is not incorrect. Not only is it something to which one is called to, the work that an individual does as a part of the Ephesians 4:11 ministry is identified by the position they hold in church leadership. The work is an office, something that they hold in the church, and something by which they are recognized.

- **A work:** Each office of the five-fold ministry has its own specific, recognizable work that goes along with its duties. Those who are in the Ephesians 4:11 ministry shouldn't be just talking about what God has called them to do; they should be doing that work.

- **A purpose:** The Ephesians 4:11 ministry works together and independently, in a more specific understanding as interdependent. It takes the entire five-fold to proclaim the Gospel as well as hold the church together, functional and running.

- **A diversity:** Each office of Ephesians 4:11 represents a different, albeit necessary, gift that exists to help accomplish the edification of the church. Not every office sounds like, looks like, or resembles a pastor. Not every office functions within a local church. In seeing the Ephesians 4:11 ministry for what it is, we need to recognize the power of opening up our own minds to the diversity and different ministries that can be found within Ephesians 4:11. There are many ways that the offices can manifest and function, and we need to be open to supporting those that are true to the Gospel, but different in mannerism and appearance.

We can't try to understand church leadership without understanding all the Ephesians 4:11 ministry, because each office of Ephesians 4:11 is a gift to the body. If we try to eliminate portions of Ephesians 4:11, declaring them obsolete or trying to absorb them into other aspects of the five-fold, we are going to lose sight of what God established for us and why He established it in the first place. What we must do, instead, is look at each office for what it is and why it exists. We will be going over the basics in this chapter, but if you want a more thorough explanation and description of the work of the five-fold ministry, I refer you to my book, *Ministry Officer Candidate School* (Righteous Pen Publications, 2026).

- **Apostle:** Meaning, "one who is sent." We discussed the apostle in the last chapter, so I will use this section to review some of that and add to it some of the more obvious facets of the work of the apostle. The primary purpose of the apostle is to go forth with the mysteries of God to establish a proper foundation for the growth and development of the church (1 Corinthians 4:1-2). This means that the apostle works to implement structure in each church. They teach, train, establish, and install leaders in every congregation (Acts 2:42, 1

Corinthians 4:17, 1 Corinthians 12:28, Philippians 2:22, 1 Timothy 1:18). Some believe apostles only have authority if they establish a congregation themselves, but we can see from the New Testament that this perspective is incorrect (Revelation 1:4). Apostles are universal authorities, which means that they have been given authority in the universal church, and do have that anywhere they go (whether it is wise to exercise such authority is a discernment call) (Ephesians 2:20). The apostle serves as God's ambassador, representing the cause of the Gospel wherever they go. They are the administrators of the church, insuring that the leaders of the church are properly equipped for their work, and that each church lacks nothing in substantial teaching and spiritual understanding (1 Timothy 4:1-9, 1 Timothy 5:22, 2 Timothy 1:6, Hebrews 6:2, 2 Peter 1:12-21, 2 Peter 2:1-22).

- **Prophet:** Meaning "one who speaks for or discerns the will of God." The work of the prophets has been seen from old, especially in the work of the Old Testament. The basic purpose of a prophet is to deliver God's message to His people and to explain and discern matters that relate to prophecy (Revelation 10:9-11). As the apostle brings structure to the church, the prophet brings the voice of God to it, setting a certain level of order and authority in the church (Amos 3:7, 1 Corinthians 14:36-40, Ephesians 3:5). Rather than being administrative, the prophet is mystical, bringing a spiritual quality and purpose to all that the church does (Ezekiel 2:1-10, Hosea 12:10). In like kind, the prophet trains other prophets and works to teach that necessary intimacy with God required for a prophet to know the voice of God as they go through different changes, seasons, and times in their own lives (1

Samuel 19:18-24). Like the apostle, the prophet is also a universal authority and operates such with discernment (Ephesians 2:19-21). Along with that discernment, the prophet is there to discern the spirits present within people and within the church (1 Corinthians 14:31-32, 1 John 4:1-3).

Scripture tells us the apostles and prophets are the foundation of the church (Ephesians 2:20). In some ways, the offices form one work together: the apostle is more administrative, and the prophet is more mystical. Working together, apostles and prophets form a powerful team that establish fundamental leadership within the church.

- **Evangelist:** Meaning "Christ-bearer." The evangelist's work is often distorted in the church today, as the first "rung" up the Ephesians 4:11 ministry ladder, and the evangelist is considered to be someone who travels around to different churches to preach. If we look at the work of the evangelist in the New Testament, assigning such work to the evangelist is incorrect (although there is nothing wrong with an evangelist traveling to different churches and preaching). They are not apostles even though they do preach beyond the borders of local churches, thus clarifying that the evangelist's office has its own work and purpose. Evangelists are called to carry the Gospel to the world, especially to the non-believer or the individual who is in a state of separation from God (Acts 8:5-6, Acts 8:27-40). The evangelist is in the category of having authority with a universal scope, without formalized church authority (meaning they are not superior to universal or local authorities but operate a position parallel to such that relates to the growth and management of the church) (Isaiah 61:1-3). They are independent, but still accountable to the church for what they teach, for which they have been thoroughly equipped for their ministry (2 Timothy 4:5).

- **Pastor:** Meaning "shepherd." The work of the pastoral office was prophesied by the Prophet Jeremiah (Jeremiah 3:15-16), and the reason we do not have a lot of New Testament references for the pastor is because the first Christians would have understood the office of the pastor to relate back to Jeremiah's prophecy. Just like the literal shepherds, pastors of the church have the job of spiritually feeding and caring for the flock entrusted to them, as well as ensuring that the flock remains together (Psalm 23:1-6, Jeremiah 12:10-17). This means that most people pastors will work with are not leaders, but lay members who need direction and guidance on spiritual living in their everyday lives. Pastors are a local authority, limited in their authority to the congregation assigned to them.

- **Teacher:** Meaning "one who teaches." The work of a teacher is pretty self-explanatory: teachers teach things (Isaiah 30:20-21, James 3:13-14). In church, they teach spiritual things to whomever God calls them to work with (Deuteronomy 4:1-10, 2 Timothy 2:22, Titus 2:4-7). A teacher may work with children, youth, or adults, and they may work in the local church, in an institution designed to educate as pertains to church, or in the universal church. Like evangelists, they may havc a universal scope of authority (beyond a local congregation), without formalized church authority (meaning they are not superior to universal or local authorities, but they operate a position parallel to such that relates to the growth and management of the church) (1 Corinthians 12:27-31).

> Much like apostles and prophets, pastors and teachers form one office together. Pastors are more about people, and teachers are more about ideas. Together, the two meet the needs that exist among people in churches, especially on a local level.

The Bible is very clear on the purpose of the Ephesians 4:11 ministry. The Ephesians 4:11 ministry exists to prepare the people of God for works of service. It is not God's will for the church to remain ignorant, nor the will of God for the church to remain stagnant. We shouldn't be going to church, listening to songs that are interpreted as being about ourselves or to puff ourselves up. No, the church is not a mutual admiration society! It exists to make sure that we are serving the church and the world, witnessing with our actions as much as with our mouths, and that we are the living, breathing change we seek to see.

A key facet to the Ephesians 4:11 ministry's operation is bringing about the unity of the church. As we discussed earlier, unity isn't something that just happens because we talk about it. The Ephesians 4:11 ministry must be working in full operation and cooperation together to bring about church unity, because within the five-fold ministry, we see universal, local, and universal scope of authority all working together. The leadership of Ephesians 4:11 covers everyone in the church: from those who don't know they are to become part of the church, to those who need to refresh their relationship with the church, to those who are in the church as lay members, to those who are in the church as leaders. Through the Ephesians 4:11 ministry, we are fully covered so the church can effectively work together as one voice, embracing each person's unique diversity, and celebrating the work and cause of the Gospel.

In the Ephesians 4:11 promise is also to bring about knowledge of the Son of God. In Jesus Christ Himself we find the entire Ephesians 4:11 ministry. He was, in His very being, an apostle, prophet, evangelist, pastor, and teacher (Matthew 10:41, Matthew 12:38, Matthew 13:57, Luke 4:14-21, John 10:11-14, Hebrews 3:1). Now we, in the church, have been given gifts that are of His very ministry and nature to help continue the work of the church (the difference being now that a leader embodies one office instead of all five). If we want to understand the ministry of Christ and His work in our lives, we need not look any further than a properly and fully functioning Ephesians 4:11 ministry. When we reach this point, where we can experience and see the knowledge of Christ as well as the unity of the church, we will come to a point of maturity. No longer will we have the headache of watching people follow deceitful leadership and spiritual falsehoods, because people will find what they need in the church. The craftiness of deceitful people who seek to distort and mislead others spiritually cannot withstand the standard established and grounded in faith, found in five offices that exist to protect and assist the church in its growth and development.

We haven't reached this point of maturity yet, which means that we still need the Ephesians 4:11 ministry. In fact, we will need the Ephesians 4:11 ministry until the One in Whom every office is found returns. The Ephesians 4:11 ministry is called to work together and build up the church in love, as we all grow together, supporting, enhancing, encouraging, and helping one another to remove our rough edges and work out all we need to as we go forward, in this work of faith, connected together.

Ephesians 4:17-24

So I tell you this, and insist on it in the Lord, that you must no longer live as the Gentiles do, in the futility of their thinking. They are darkened in their understanding and separated from the life of

God because of the ignorance that is in them due to the hardening of their hearts. Having lost all sensitivity, they have given themselves over to sensuality so as to indulge in every kind of impurity, with a continual lust for more.

You, however, did not come to know Christ that way. Surely you heard of Him and were taught in Him in accordance with the truth that is in Jesus. You were taught, with regard to your former way of life, to put off your old self, which is being corrupted by its deceitful desires; to be made new in the attitude of your minds; and to put on the new self, created to be like God in true righteousness and holiness.

(Related Bible references: Psalm 51:10, Ezekiel 11:19, Acts 17:30, Acts 26:18, Romans 1:21, Romans 6:6, Romans 8:13, Romans 12:2, Galatians 3:27, Galatians 4:8, Galatians 5:19, Colossians 1:21, 1 Thessalonians 4:4, Hebrews 7:26, 1 Peter 4:3, Jude 1:4)

The Apostle Paul devotes a lot of his writings to Gentile matters, because he predominately worked with churches composed primarily of Gentiles. What is perhaps most noticeable about how he begins this statement is that he does not, any longer, identify the individuals he is writing to as "Gentiles." He does not say they are Jewish, but he clarifies now they are in Christ, and that means that they are something new, something different. This means that, having come out of the world, one of the primary differences between those who are in church and those who are not is how they behave and live in their everyday lives.

It doesn't sound that deep or fascinating to think that God cares about our everyday lives, but the truth is that He does. He cares about them so much, in fact, that the remainder of the book of Ephesians is about things we encounter in our everyday existences. We talk so much about big things or the issues we perceive to be big and important that we forget that the darkness of our past understanding has been illuminated by Christ, and that we have been turned away from the hardness and impurities of the world we came from. We are not people driven by every sensual lust, whether it is a drive for power, a drive for physical things, for physical pleasures, or for aspirations. We are moved and driven by the Spirit, turning away from the ignorance that once dominated our drives and our purpose for living.

Coming to know Christ should not be a part of such a drive. We should not be in Christ because we aspire to gain things or gain some kind of prestige from it. Rather, the relationship we have with Christ is known by the Spirit. We are taught of Him, by Him, and about Him. He shows us that we are dead to our old lives, which we are putting aside, as we change our minds and our attitudes, and we put on the new self, renewed by the inner man. As we go about our lives and we walk more deeply with Christ, we can see why we were created in the first place: to exemplify the ways of God, living as He would desire, in all righteousness (right living) and holiness.

Ephesians 4:25-32

Therefore each of you must put off falsehood and speak truthfully to his neighbor, for we are all members of one body. "In your anger do not sin:" Do not let the sun go down while you are still angry, and do not give the devil a foothold. He who has been stealing must steal no longer, but must work, doing something useful with his own hands, that he may have something to share with those in need.

Do not let any unwholesome talk come out of your mouths, but only what is helpful for building others up according to their needs, that it may benefit those who listen. And do not grieve the Holy Spirit of God, with Whom you were sealed for the day of redemption. Get rid of all bitterness, rage and anger, brawling and slander, along with every form of malice. Be kind and compassionate to one

another, forgiving each other, just as in Christ God forgave you.

(Related Bible references: Leviticus 19:17, Deuteronomy 5:19, Psalm 4:4, Micah 6:8, Zechariah 8:16, Matthew 6:14-15, Matthew 12:31-32, Matthew 18:35, Mark 11:25, Acts 20:35, Romans 12:5, 2 Corinthians 2:10, Colossians 3:8-9, Colossians 3:12-13, Colossians 4:6, 1 Thessalonians 4:11, 1 Thessalonians 5:19, 2 Thessalonians 3:10, Titus 3:2, James 3:10, 1 Peter 3:8)

What does it mean to be righteous and holy? The denominations of the ages have tried to answer this question by creating long lists of rules and regulations to be upheld by members. These various traditions of men have all disagreed with each other, and most codes are rejected by later generations. Rather than creating a big, long list of guidelines, God has given to us some general guidelines to go by in our conduct with others. This makes it so that our interactions with others are not strained, nor are they so super-spiritual that other people can't relate to us. I often speak about finding balance between things and the importance of discovering middle ground, which I believe the Bible encourages us to find. This passage provides us with the middle ground that we need to seek when dealing with other people. Our lives cannot be a long string of Bible verses spoken in every moment of the day, and the Bible recognizes that much of our faith needs to be lived out rather than relying on speech to convey what we desire. As a result, the Bible advises us to speak without falsehood and with truth to our neighbor. Whether we have a Christian neighbor or a non-Christian neighbor doesn't matter. We are all members of the body of Christ, and when one of us takes up lying or falsehoods, such behavior reflects negatively on the entire church. We have all met someone who refuses to go to church or refuses to talk about Christ because of how that one person who claimed to be a Christian behaved. If we follow these precepts – especially the one against lying – we won't be that person who turned off someone to the

Lord.

We are also strongly commanded to control our emotions, especially our anger. Even though we don't often think of it, the Bible reveals much to us about people's feelings, even when they don't know how to handle them properly. Regardless, anger is not spoken of as being a sin anywhere in the Bible. The Bible recognizes that we, as human beings, will have different feelings from time to time and that there is nothing wrong with having them. The numb, indifferent state many preachers claim is God's will for us is, in fact, not what He desires for us. We have an expanse of feelings that are given to us as indicators of how we react to situations, and those reveal much about us as people. They reveal strengths as well as weaknesses, areas we need to work on as much as areas that we are victorious in, and they are things that we must learn to recognize and identify within ourselves.

This does not mean that our emotions should control our lives, however. If we have emotional states and outbursts that are completely out of control, we are going to be all-too tempted to sin in our lives. Undisciplined emotions lead to sin, because they lead to selfishness and entitlement. The way we can avoid this is to resolve our feelings, however is most productive and without harming others, as quickly as possible. Before the day passes, we should work through our feelings from that day. Rather than allowing our feelings to fester within us, we should avoid giving the enemy a foothold through them by resolving them and finding solutions to our situations.

Christians are called to be productive. There should never be a Christian individual who does not have something to do. We are called to attend to our work, whatever that is, and provide for ourselves and for those who are in need. Stealing is unacceptable, as is laziness.

The last major aspect of conduct that is addressed in this chapter is all about how we speak to one another. Coupled with the self-control needed to manage and control our emotions is the needed watch over the way that we speak, one to another. There is a marked difference between speaking the truth to help someone realize a truth and just speaking something that might be the truth to offend someone else. We can tell the truth all day long and do it for the wrong reasons, and doing so makes whatever we say wrong, no matter how factual it might be. What we say should be for a benefit, and that benefit is to the hearer. We should never just be speaking to benefit ourselves or to boast in our own agendas. Speech has a purpose, and that purpose is to bless and encourage.

It's interesting the command to avoid grieving the Holy Spirit is mentioned right in the middle of several verses pertaining to speech, improper speech, rage, brawling, and anger. This is not an accident, not by any stretch of the imagination. We try to speculate what it means to grieve the Spirit and what that unforgivable sin is (Matthew 12:31-32), but the truth is that it relates to blaspheming, or speaking against the Spirit of God, and all the Holy Spirit stands for. It is accomplished whenever we act out of rage, brawling, and anger in sin against another person. Grieving the Spirit comes forth whenever we claim to be a believer, but we do, act, and say to the contrary of just what that means.

Chapter four's final words to us are of forgiveness (Matthew 6:15). Too often, we allow our feelings, our opinions, and our thoughts to allow a certain bitterness and unforgiveness to nestle within our hearts and grow into a place of resentment. God, no matter how justified He might have been to be angry and bitter toward us, was rather kind and compassionate. He extended His love and mercy, calling us gently home to Him, to the church, where we are nurtured and cared for, by His grace. He forgave us through Christ, even though we didn't deserve it. Thus, even when every feeling we have makes us want to hold on...makes us want to feel justified in resentment and hostility...even when we have been seriously wronged...we are to forgive each other with the same love and grace, just as in Christ, God has forgiven us.

Chapter Five

The Mystery of the Church Veiled in the Ordinary (Ephesians Chapter 5)

Key verses

- **Verses 1-2:** *Be imitators of God, therefore, as dearly loved children and live a life of love, just as Christ loved us and gave Himself up for us as a fragrant offering and sacrifice to God.*

- **Verses 8-10:** *For you were once darkness, but now you are light in the Lord. Live as children of light (for the fruit of the light consists in all goodness, righteousness and truth) and find out what pleases the Lord.*

- **Verse 21:** *Submit to one another out of reverence for Christ.*

- **Verses 31-33:** *"For this reason a man will leave his father and mother and be united to his wife, and the two will become one flesh." This is a profound mystery – but I am talking about Christ and the church. However, each one of you also must love his wife as he loves himself, and the wife must respect her husband.*

Words and phrases to know

- **Imitators:** From the Greek word *mimetes* which means "an imitator."[1]

- **Fragrant offering:** From two Greek words: *prosphora* which means "the act of offering, a bringing to; that which is offered, a gift, a present. In the NT a sacrifice, whether bloody or not: offering for sin, expiatory offering"[2] and *euodia* which means "a sweet smell, fragrance; a fragrant or sweet smelling thing, incense, on odour or something sweet smelling; metaph. a thing well pleasing to God."[3]

- **Sacrifice:** From the Greek word *thusia* which means "a sacrifice, victim."[4]

- **Sexual immorality:** From the Greek word *porneia* which means "illicit sexual intercourse (as in, prostitution, particularly temple prostitution[5]); metaph. the worship of idols."[6]

- **Impurity:** From the Greek word *akatharsia* which means "uncleanness."[7]

- **Greed:** From the Greek word *pleonexia* which means "greedy desire to have more, covetousness, avarice."[8]

- **Obsenity:** From the Greek word *aischrotes* which means "obscenity, filthiness."[9]

- **Foolish talk:** From the Greek word *morologia* which means "foolish talking."[10]

- **Coarse joking:** From the Greek word *eutrapelia* which means "pleasantry, humor, facetiousness; in a bad sense."[11]

- **Thanksgiving:** From the Greek word *eucharistia* which means "thankfulness; the giving of thanks."[12]

- **Idolater:** From the Greek word *eidololatres* which means "a worshipper of false gods, a idolater; a covetous man as a worshipper of Mammon."[13]

- **Fruitless deeds of darkness:** From three Greek words: *akarpos* which means "metaph. without fruit, barren, not yielding what it ought to yield,"[14] *ergon* which means "business, employment, that which any one is occupied; any product whatever, any thing accomplished by hand, art, industry, or mind; an act, deed, thing done: the idea of working is emphasized in opp. to that which is less than work,"[15] and *skotos* which means "darkness; metaph. of ignorance respecting divine things and human duties, and the accompanying ungodliness and immorality, together with their consequent misery in hell, persons in whom darkness becomes visible and holds sway."[16]

- **Expose:** From the Greek word *elegcho* which means "to convict, refute, confute; to find fault with, correct."[17]

- **Drunk:** From the Greek word *methusko* which means "to intoxicate, make drunk; to get drunk, become intoxicated."[18]

- **Wine:** From the Greek word *oinos* which means "wine; metaph. fiery wine of God's wrath."[19]

- **Filled:** From the Greek word *pleroo* which means "to make full, to fill up, i.e. to fill to the full; to render full, i.e. to complete."[20]

- **Psalms:** From the Greek word *psalmos* which means "a striking, twanging."[21]

- **Hymns:** From the Greek word *humnos* which means "a song in tithe praise of gods, heroes, conquerors; a sacred song, hymn."[22]

- **Spiritual songs:** From two Greek words: *pneumatikos* which means "relating to the human spirit, or rational soul, as part of the man which is akin to God and serves as his instrument or organ; belonging to a spirit, or a being higher than man but inferior to God; belonging to the Divine Spirit; pertaining to the wind or breath; windy, exposed to the wind, blowing"[23] and *ode* which means "a song, lay, ode."[24]

- **Sing:** From the Greek word *ado* which means "to the praise of anyone, to sing."[25]

- **Make music:** From the Greek word *psallo* which means "to pluck off, pull out; to cause to vibrate by touching, to twang."[26]

- **Submit:** From the Greek word *hupotasso* which means "to arrange under, to subordinate; to subject, put in subjection; to subject one's self, obey; to submit to one's control; to yield to one's admonition or advice; to obey, be subject."[27]

- **Wives:** From the Greek word *gune* which means "a woman of any age, whether a virgin, or married, or a widow; a wife."[28]

- **Head:** From the Greek word *kephale* which means "the head, both of men and often of animals. Since the loss of the head destroys life, this word is used in the phrases relating to capital and extreme punishment; metaph. anything prominent."[29]

- **Husbands:** From the Greek word *aner* which means "with reference to sex, of a male, of a husband, of a betrothed or future husband; with reference to age, and to distinguish an adult man from a boy; any male; used generically of a group of both men and women."[30]

- **Gave Himself up:** From two Greek words: *paradidomi* which means "to give into the hands (of another); to give over into (one's) power or use; to commit, to commend; to deliver verbally; to permit allow"[31] and *heautou* which means "himself, herself, itself, themselves."[32]

- **Cleansing:** From the Greek word *hagiazo* which means "to render or acknowledge, or to be venerable or hallow; to separate from profane things and dedicate to God; to purify."[33]

- **Water:** From the Greek word *hudor* which means "water."[34]

- **Word:** From the Greek word *rhema* which means "that which is or has been uttered by the living voice, thing spoken, word; subject matter of speech, thing spoken of."[35]

- **Radiant:** From the Greek word *endoxos* which means "held in good or in great esteem, of high repute."[36]

- **Stain:** From the Greek word *spilos* which means "a spot; a fault, moral blemish."[37]

- **Wrinkle:** From the Greek word: *rhutis* which means "a wrinkle."[38]

- **Blemish:** From the Greek word *amomos* which means "without blemish; morally: without blemish, faultless, unblameable."[39]

- **Bodies:** From the Greek word *soma* which means "the body both of men or animals; the bodies of plants and of stars (heavenly bodies); is used of a (large or small) number of men closely united into one society, or family as it were; a social, ethical, mystical body; that which casts a shadow as distinguished from the shadow itself."[40]

- **Profound:** From the Greek word *megas* which means "great; predicated of rank, as belonging to persons, eminent for ability, virtue, authority, power, things esteemed highly for their importance: of great moment, of great weight, importance, a thing to be highly esteemed for its excellence: excellent; splendid, prepared on a grand scale, stately; great things."[41]

- **Respect:** From the Greek word *phobeo* which means "to put to flight by terrifying (to scare away)."[42]

Ephesians 5:1-7

Be imitators of God, therefore, as dearly loved children and live a life of love, just as Christ loved us and gave Himself up for us as a fragrant offering and sacrifice to God.

But among you there must not be even a hint of sexual immorality, or of any kind of impurity, or of greed, because these are improper for God's holy people. Nor should there be obscenity, foolish talk or coarse joking, which are out of place, but rather thanksgiving. For of this you can be sure: No immoral, impure or greedy person – such a man is an idolater – has any inheritance in the Kingdom of Christ and of God. Let no one deceive you with empty words, for because of such things God's wrath comes on those who are disobedient. Therefore do not be partners with them.

(Related Bible references: Psalm 69:30, Psalm 95:2, Psalm 100:4-5, Proverbs 26:26, Isaiah 51:3, Jeremiah 9:6, Malachi 3:8-12, Luke 6:36, Acts 15:29, Romans 15:16, 1 Corinthians 1:4, 1 Corinthians 5:11, 1 Corinthians 6:9, 1 Corinthians 16:14, 2 Corinthians 2:15, 2 Corinthians 4:2, 2 Corinthians 6:14, Galatians 5:19-21, Philippians 2:17, Colossians 2:4-8, Colossians 3:5-8, 1 Thessalonians 4:3, 1 Thessalonians 5:18, 1 Peter 2:5)

The first half of Ephesians chapter 5 picks up where chapter 4 left off. We're detailing further into the realities of everyday life, of things that are not seemingly supernatural or exciting, but deal with how we, as people, conduct ourselves with other people. When most people teach about Ephesians, this particular section of Ephesians doesn't tend to be what they focus on. They are interested to talk about men and women or spiritual warfare, making it sound like something right out of a *Star Wars* chronicle. We like to get big and dramatic when talking about the enemy and about the way the enemy works, with a big, booming voice that commands everyone's attention.

If we listen to the wrong people, we can get the idea that walking with God is nothing more than a big, intense spiritual high. In fact, there are many people who move from one spiritual experience to the other, just seeking and waiting for something to happen. It's always about the next vision, or the next word from above, or the next supernatural occurrence, which they cannot live without. These are people, who I call "supernatural chasers," who have never learned the value or principle of walking with God in the experience of the ordinary.

I believe this is a key principle of the spiritual life that we don't often consider, nor regard, in the way we often should. We tend to assume that the life of the church was one big spiritual park amusement ride. In reading the incredible things that happened in the book of Acts, we think every weekly service was miracle after miracle after miracle. The letters of the Apostles Paul, Peter, James, John, and the book of Jude all prove that life in the church settled down after a while. The members of the church were left to deal with everyday, ordinary things, things which brought the realities of their spiritual lives into focus in a real way. While I don't doubt or question that awesome and amazing miracles occurred all throughout New Testament times and beyond (or that they are still happening today, because of course they are), I don't think that they happened every time someone turned around, as we assume that they did. At some point in time, the New Testament church settled into their relationship with God and had to learn to recognize God in the details, in the ordinary and boring aspects of everything that they did in life.

That's why Ephesians spends so much time on our everyday conduct with one another. The church was identified for its supernatural workings, but it was noted in a much bigger way for how its people lived and conducted themselves, and for how those little things witnessed to those around them. Yes, God cares about our ordinary and our everyday, even in the form of our interactions with others, even in the concept of something as commonplace as marriage and family, and yes, especially in our thoughts, conduct, and ability to walk in self-control.

Being imitators of God is about a lot more than just being powerful and supernatural. Have you ever considered just what it means to be modeling God in our conduct and our behavior? The work of God in our lives reflects far more patience, love, and endurance than it does with anything else. Being a model of the love of God that has transformed us is about more than giving someone a Bible verse or randomly praying for someone when they have an issue. It is a lifestyle, a worldview, a way of looking at others and at ourselves that brings us to a place where we can finally see the bigger picture. Life is bigger than the moments that upset us, than the people who irritate us, then even the things that break our hearts. Having the ability to look at things with love and look beyond ourselves and the pain and offenses we encounter helps us so we can rise above them. It is about sacrifice, even sacrificing that which is most important to us. In offering that fragrant offering of ourselves before the Lord (Romans 15:16, 2 Corinthians 2:15, Philippians 2:17, 1 Peter 2:5), we give to Him our lives, being willing to lay them down for what is truly best in the eyes of eternity. It was God Who gave us His only Son that we might live, because God knew in the long run what the outcome would be and what was most important therein. We too, then, as imitators of God, are willing to do what is needed in love, seeing the bigger picture and bigger promise that lies just ahead.

The next course of discussion that the Apostle Paul moves on to are three things that there should not even be a hint, or trace of, among the churches. These three things are:

- **Sexual immorality:** We tend to use the term "sexual immorality" quite loosely in the church today, often in ways that it is not properly defined in Scripture. This is one of those passages, of which the Greek refers to prostitution, or more spiritually put, idolatry. Prostitution was not just a social custom, but one that related to pagan rites, and participating in a sexual rite with a prostitute would have been, therefore, idolatry. To participate in a sexual pagan rite was to unite oneself to the demonic, and to demons. Such a practice would have been seriously addressed because it was not just one that was physical practice, but a spiritual one, as well.

- **Impurity:** Impurity is the state or manifestation of something being considered impure, thus created by a pollutant of some sort. Impurity in this particular context most likely refers to sin, to the church being rendered impure because of sin among the brethren. This means that sin must be taken seriously, and that we should make the effort to eliminate sin among us within the church.

- **Greed:** Greed has a lot of manifestations and many repercussions, all of which are harmful to the body of Christ. If someone in the church is greedy and taking more for themselves than is reasonably necessary, that means they are taking away from the provisions that should be there for someone else who is in need. Greed leads to an uneven distribution of provision, causing lack, which should not exist when we consider that God has promised provision to all who are His people (Malachi 3:8-12).

These three things are described as being improper (inappropriate) for God's people. If we are to live according to our own precepts, then we should follow them, even when confronted with common temptations. Sex that leads one away from God, idolatry, sin, and greed are all common temptations known to mankind, which is why they are specifically stated here. It is not foreign to assume that they were, most likely, issues for people who were right there, in the church. Thinking that greed, sexual idolatry, or sin aren't as serious as something else that one could be doing is a common thought process that enables people to stay right where they are, committing those same sins, time and time again. Yet, we are reminded that these things should not be a part of our lives, nor of our church. The passage goes on to remind us that there are other things that should not be a part of our conduct, including:

- **Obscenity:** A reference to talk that is somehow considered shameful or improper among the church. In other words, it is the suggestion in some way (it can be either through word or action) of something inappropriate for church behavior or discussion, such as a sexually suggestive song done by a choir or content that is inappropriately preached from the pulpit or discussed in church. It can also extend to sexual harassment or otherwise unwanted sexual discussion or contact among people (where one party is not interested in such).

- **Foolish talk:** Literally means "silly talk," or talk that doesn't have much relevance.

- **Coarse joking:** There is nothing wrong with having a good sense of humor, but there is something wrong with telling jokes that are at another person's expense. It is not right to make fun of other people, to interact in a manner that is disrespectful or coarse, or to tell jokes that demean ethnic groups, races, genders, or other individuals in general.

What we should fill our mouths and our conducts with are thanksgivings. We should be people so full of praise to God and gratitude for the things that He has done for us and the things that we have that there is no room to demean, insult, or belittle other people. This is conduct befitting for a Christian, that echoes so much purpose and warmth, even in the ordinary, that others can see we are transformed (Psalm 69:30, Psalm 95:2, Psalm 100:4-5, Isaiah 51:3, 1 Corinthians 1:4).

We are warned against deception, and we are warned against partnerships with those who are not walking as they should with God (Proverbs 26:26, Jeremiah 9:6, 2 Corinthians 4:2). The three main signs, all of which are compared to idolatry, are the same as was mentioned above: Sexual idolatry, impurity, and greed. These are things by which someone cannot inherit the Kingdom, because they are all instances where individuals are chasing after things more than they are chasing after God. We should not follow those who deceive themselves that such are acceptable, nor should we be people who are deceived by such. Rather, we should avoid alliances with those who are clearly lost and not seeking to find their way.

Ephesians 5:8-20

For you were once darkness, but now you are light in the Lord. Live as children of light (for the fruit of the light consists in all goodness, righteousness and truth) and find out what pleases the Lord. Have nothing to do with the fruitless deeds of darkness, but rather expose them. For it is shameful even to mention what the disobedient do in secret. But everything exposed by the light becomes visible, for it is light that makes everything visible. This is why it is said:

"Wake up, O sleeper,
rise from the dead,
and Christ will shine on you."

Be very careful, then, how you live – not as unwise but as wise, making the most of every opportunity, because the days are evil. Therefore do not be foolish, but understand what the Lord's will is. Do

not get drunk on wine, which leads to debauchery. Instead, be filled with the Spirit. Speak to one another with psalms, hymns and spiritual songs. Sing and make music in your heart to the Lord, always giving thanks to God the Father for everything, in the Name of our Lord Jesus Christ.

(Related Bible references: Psalm 143:10, Proverbs 5:20-23, Proverbs 28:23, Isaiah 5:11, Isaiah 26:19, Isaiah 52:11, Habakkuk 2:5, Matthew 5:16, John 3:20, John 8:12, Acts 2:4, Acts 26:18, Romans 12:2, Romans 13:11-12, 1 Corinthians 4:5, 1 Corinthians 14:15, Galatians 5:22-23, Colossians 3:15-16, Colossians 4:5, 1 Thessalonians 5:18, 2 Thessalonians 3:6, 2 Timothy 1:10, Titus 1:13, James 5:13, 1 Peter 2:9, Revelation 3:19)

Recalling what had been discussed in an earlier chapter, all of us were once in darkness. We were all in a place where we didn't understand better and we didn't know better. The difference between then and now is that we do know better, and we must now live as children of the light, reflecting principles that are different from those of darkness. We shouldn't be trying to cover up the things that people do which are shameful or contrary to God, because such is to participate in darkness. As we walk with the Lord, He reveals more of Himself to us, and we discover more and more what is pleasing to Him. Something we might not have even considered doing years ago we now know we must do in obedience, and now there are things we would never imagine that we should do. Our understanding of God's will grows with us, and as we discern more of that will, we come to a place where we are able to walk in that will in a better way.

This means we must keep our heads clear, walking in the day, waking from our sleep and making ourselves aware of the things of which we must take note. We should avoid foolishness and foolish behavior, including drunkenness and intoxication (using any substance, including alcohol or drugs, both prescription and non-prescription), because that literally leads to excessive behavior, rioting, disorder, and behavior that is contrary to the calling that we have in Christ (Proverbs 5:20-23, Isaiah 5:11, Habakkuk 2:5). Instead of being filled with intoxicants, we should be filled with the Spirit, so full that there is no room for false or misleading things, and that what comes forth from our mouths is of blessing to God: songs, hymns, spiritual songs, things that sing from within us, and come out in the form of our never-ending praise (Colossians 3:15-16). We give thanks continually, recognizing from whence it has come, and seeing praise as a key to our victory in where we are going (1 Thessalonians 5:18).

Ephesians 5:21-33

Submit to one another out of reverence for Christ.

Wives, submit to your husbands as to the Lord. For the husband is the head of the wife as Christ is the head of the church, His body, of which He is the Savior. Now as the church submits to Christ, so also wives should submit to their husbands in everything.

Husbands, love your wives, just as Christ love the church and gave Himself up for her to make her holy, cleansing her by the washing with the water through the Word, and to present her to Himself as a radiant church, without stain or wrinkle or any other blemish, but holy and blameless. In this same way, husbands ought to love their wives as their own bodies. He who loves his wife loves himself. After all, no one ever hated his own body, but he feeds and cares for it, just as Christ does the church – for we are members of His body. "For this reason a man will leave his father and mother and be united to his wife, and the two will become one flesh." This is a profound mystery – but I am talking about Christ and the church. However, each one of you also must love his wife as he loves himself, and the wife must respect her husband.

(Related Bible references: Genesis 2:18,21-24, Genesis 16:9, 2 Chronicles 30:8, Job 22:21, Psalm 45:13, Proverbs 3:6, Matthew 19:5, Matthew 20:26, Mark 10:43, Acts 2:18, Romans 12:5, Romans 13:5, 2 Corinthians 11:2, Galatians 1:4, Philippians 2:3, Colossians 1:22-26, Colossians 3:18-19, Titus 2:14, Hebrews 10:22, Hebrews 13:12, 1 Peter 3:1-7, 1 Peter 5:5)

The last section of Ephesians 5 is probably one of the most controversial passages of all Scripture. It has been preached up and down, in and out, and it seems like with each passing generation, we get further and further away from where we are supposed to be. A lot of these controversies could be resolved if we step back and stop trying to read so many of these passages in the flesh. Up to this point in chapter 5, we have been receiving practical, every day, ordinary advice about interacting with each other, and the truth is that a large part of this passage also reflects the everyday and the ordinary. God, however, flips the script here and shows us something deep and powerful in something as boring and ordinary as marriage.

Marriage was, in ancient times, regarded as much like it is today: a societal norm. People were expected, once they reached a certain age, to get married. Having children was a must in agrarian societies that relied on children to serve as free farm labor. Male children were required to insure that property remained in families and were given far preferential treatment over girls. Women were regarded as property and seen as a vehicle to bring heirs into the world. Enter in one of the most radical statements found in the Bible, before the discussion on marriage even begins: Submit to one another out of reverence for Christ.

Let's start by saying outright that there's nothing wrong with submission. It might feel like a dirty word in our mouths, but it's actually very important. We understand it when it is to our benefit (or more aptly, how to use it for manipulative purposes), but it gets much harder when it costs more of us than we want to give. Submission is a principle by which we don't esteem ourselves more highly than we ought. No matter what our position is in the church, in the world, or in the home, none of us is any better than anyone else in the sight of God. Being a spiritual people means that we do not ignore, nor overlook, the things God tries to teach us in the ordinary aspects of our lives. The entire reason that God cares about our ordinary, everyday, even boring is because there are things there within that reveal to us about God's nature. If we start to understand types and shadows less as large things and instead as the small ways that God reveals Himself to us in little bits and pieces, we can see that God is revealing Himself to us every day, in things that are familiar, and we can recognize. This is why the call to submit one to another in church is so important. We are called to learn from one another, serve each other, and remain humble, no matter how lofty or important we may be to those in the eyesight of this world.

Submission is not, as is clear here, a principle that is unique or special for marriage (Genesis 16:9, 2 Chronicles 30:8, Job 22:21, Proverbs 3:6, Romans 13:5, Philippians 2:3, 1 Peter 5:5). That little sentence, so often ignored in the discussions on marriage, is what makes the entire passage make sense and clarify its intent and meaning. By mentioning the command for the entire church to submit, one to another, the Apostle Paul is hinting to all of us that this lesson is about Christ and the church, not just about men, women, and marriage. Unfortunately, through the years, we have focused so much on only one side of view pertaining to this passage that we have completely mis-stepped, ignored, and refused to accept what is being taught to us.

The teachings on Biblical submission are often taught through the lens of patriarchal culture: men are the head of the household, women and children are the property of the men, and women are, by extension, subordinate to men in all possible ways. The passage, in its literal setting, was a reference to the Roman Codes, a societal household setup by which male land owners held full responsibility and rites over everyone in their domain, including women, children, and slaves. By modern understanding, it might seem outdated, even archaic in one form or another. It's easy to suggest we should just sweep it under the rug, for a different time and place. But if we want to understand the passage's contents, it's essential we understand where and when it was from, as well as the way in which it was extremely progressive for its time.

It's important to consider everything just mentioned. The passage was written in Greek, not English. It was written to a Greek-speaking audience who was antithetical to the government's system. Its underlying message is also the most important thing: Christ and the church. Stepping back to start with these basics helps us understand it, instead of automatically assuming it endorses traditions of power and control, assuming women are seen as inferior to men. No matter how much people who endorse a traditional understanding of this passage might try to talk around what I just said, that is the root of the understanding. They do not see the beauty of submission, the relationship between Christ and the church. They don't recognize Christ does not force anyone to be a part of His church, nor does He lead us with abuse and a dominant spirit. What Christ did for the church was die for it, submit His life to the Father's will and surrender Himself that humanity might be saved. Christ performed the ultimate act of submission, not the ultimate act of control.

This is the very essence of what is wrong with the way people interpret Ephesians 5:22-33. They teach that women should allow their husbands to abuse their bodies, to constantly make themselves available for servitude or sexual favors even if they are in pain or physically incapacitated, that they should have no voice in marriages, and that they should blindly follow and do whatever their husbands want, whether it is right.

Those who teach this approach also encourage men to be leaders, to be insensitive and ignorant to the needs that their wives have, to stifle their voices, and that being a "godly man" means behaving in an abusive and brutish way.

The word "submit" is not even found in Ephesians 5:22. The literal Greek rendering of the passage is, "And wives to their husbands," which means that the word "submit" in Ephesians 5:21 is where the word "submit" comes from. This means that Ephesians 5:22 refers to the mutual submission present among believers, back in Ephesians 5:21. There are a few important reasons for this. The first is that women were encouraged to regard their husbands as they regarded any man in the church. This was a radical departure from cultural ideas about landowners, reminding them that they were not entitled to do whatever they wanted without consequence. Husbands were not, contrary to popular societal belief, better than any other man. They were not entitled to treat their wives any which way, and the treatment a woman could expect to receive from her husband should model that of Christ, meaning he should not behave toward her as if she were his property.

The virtue of this passage elevates the status of the woman above property and the man above societal conditioning that dictates to him what it means to be a good husband. The word "head" in verse 23 is the Greek word *kephale*, which does not mean head as in authority, but the head as in originator, or founder. We know from Genesis 2:18, 21-24 that man and woman were originally created as one, and that woman was taken out of man:

Then the LORD God said, "It is not good for the man to be alone. I will make a helper [in the sense of a partner or ally; the word does not imply subordinate status; see Ps. 79:9] who is right for [is suitable for; corresponds with] him..."So the LORD God caused the man to sleep very deeply [a deep sleep to fall on the man/Adam], and while he was asleep, God removed one of the man's ribs [or sides]. Then God closed up the man's skin at the place where he took the rib [or side]. The LORD God used the rib [or side] from the man to make [build; construct] a woman, and then he brought the woman to the man.

And the man said,

"Now, this is someone whose bones came from my bones,
whose body came from my body [At last, this is bone of my bones and flesh of my flesh].
I will call her [She will be called] 'woman [Hebrew 'ishshah],'
because she was taken out of man [Hebrew 'ish]."

So a man will leave his father and mother [in the sense of a new primary loyalty] and be united with his wife, and the two will become one body [flesh]. (EXB)

The passage never meant to imply that a woman was under the control or dominance of a man, but that she was a part of him, and he of her, and that the two of them need to work together to complete the covenant, the promise of marriage that makes it work in the eyes of God. In marriage, man and woman come back together in that original oneness, that original unity, as God has put them together. It's more than a marriage license that decides if a couple is married, and it is completely possible that a couple can be married legally but not united from the heavenly perspective. If a couple is not working toward these things and mutually striving for the balance of oneness, then they aren't really married in the truest sense of cooperation and purpose. (This is teaching for another time, but something that we should keep in mind when we consider these different concepts.)

It should be obvious now, by this point in the book, that's not what God is saying to us, at all, in this passage. If anything, I believe it is reinforcing a principle of mutual submission and teaching us that submission is not static. If you are in Christ, then you are called to be a servant (Matthew 20:26, Mark 10:43, Acts 2:18), and that means wives should serve their husbands and husbands should also be serving their wives. Spouses, regardless of gender, should serve each other. Marriage is not a one-dimensional experience where one fulfills one constant role and another a different one. In fact, marriage is extremely multi-dimensional. There isn't one situation where one person always defers to the will of another one, because that destroys the concept of working together and walking in agreement. If you are truly submitting yourself to God, that makes you a servant, not a boss. If we are standing before God as honorable people, and submitting to Christ, Who is the true Head of every church and every household, then we are learning how to walk in love, and love one another. That means that there will be times when a wife will need to yield to her husband's situation or position, and there will be times when a husband will have to yield to his wife's position. When a husband is told by God that his position is to love his wife as Christ loved the church, that is an act of submission, of dying to Himself, to love her rightly and properly. This means that both partners in the marriage need to submit themselves to the other. They need to look at themselves first, respect one another, and care enough about their marriage to realize it isn't all about them. This is how we continue to uphold Christian values in a marriage, without it becoming about power and control.

Marriage is a type and a reality, all in and of itself. It is something that is amazing and a realization of love, something where two people come together in the walk of covenant in a true sense. Spouses both give something up to be together and gain something even greater. The passage isn't about who makes more money than who or who stays home with the kids while who works. It's not about society, and maybe that is, in essence, the point. We need to get society out of our marriages and our arrangements. The Apostle Paul was using marriage to teach us of the great mystery of Christ and the church, which is called a "great mystery" because it is something that, no matter how much we might try, we will only understand in types and shadows this side of heaven. That doesn't mean we shouldn't try, but it does mean that it is something so unfathomable, it is beyond our full comprehension. We will never fully understand the incredible grace, power, and yes, relationship that comes from walking out our lives with another person, and the covenant that results.

If God is trying to teach us something through marriage about the church, then that means that there are things in church that are parallel to marriage. The guidelines are the same, and we should embrace them, both at home and in church:

- Mutual submission of one to another
- A spirit of reverence
- A yielding Spirit to our Head, Christ
- A willingness to serve one another
- Love as Christ loved the church
- Washing in baptism
- Glory and splendor without evil, sin, or any wrong thing in it
- Loving as we love our own bodies (as ourselves)
- Becoming one

All these things are commands not just for married people, but for the church, as well. When married couples approach marriage with the right attitude, which is addressed here – walking in love, yielding to Christ and to one another, serving one another, striving to become one, and striving to live together without sin between the two – we see the type active, a relationship that reflects Christian precept and the values that He desires us to have one to another, and with Him. When the church upholds Christian principles for marriage and also looks to these different, ordinary things as a model for who we should be – we will see both the church – and marriage – change.

Chapter Six

The Church's Endurance in the World (Ephesians Chapter 6)

Key verses

- **Verse 1:** *Children, obey your parents in the Lord, for this is right.*

- **Verse 4:** *Fathers, do not exasperate your children; instead, bring them up in the training and instruction of the Lord.*

- **Verses 5-6:** *Slaves, obey your earthly masters with respect and fear, and with sincerity of heart, just as you would obey Christ. Obey them not only to win their favor when their eye is on you, but like slaves of Christ, doing the will of God from your heart.*

- **Verse 9:** *And masters, treat your slaves in the same way. Do not threaten them, since you know that He Who is both their Master and yours is in heaven, and there is no favoritism with Him.*

- **Verses 11-12:** *Put on the full armor of God so that you can take your stand against the devil's schemes. For our struggle is not against flesh and blood, but against the rulers, against the authorities, against the powers of this dark world* *and against the spiritual forces of evil in the heavenly realms.*

- **Verse 18:** *And pray in the Spirit on all occasions with all kinds of prayers and requests. With this in mind, be alert and always keep on praying for all the saints.*

Words and phrases to know

- **Children:** From the Greek word *teknon* which means "offspring, children."[1]

- **Obey:** From the Greek word *hupakouo* which means "to listen, to harken; to harken to a command."[2]

- **Parents:** From the Greek word *goneus* which means "fathers, parent, the parents."[3]

- **Right:** From the Greek word *dikaios* which means "righteous, observing divine laws."[4]

- **Fathers:** From the Greek word *pater* which means "generator or male ancestor; metaph. the originator and transmitter of anything, one who stands in a father's place and looks after another in a paternal way, a title of honor; God is called the Father."[5]

- **Exasperate:** From the Greek word *parorgizo* which means "to rouse to wrath, to provoke, exasperate, anger."[6]

- **Slaves:** From the Greek word *doulos* which means "a slave, bondman, man of servile condition; a servant, attendant."[7]

- **Masters:** From the Greek word *kurios* which means he to whom a person or thing belongs, about which he has power of deciding; master, lord."[8]

- **Sincerity of heart:** From two Greek words: *haplotes* which means "singleness, simplicity, sincerity, mental honesty; not self-seeking, openness of heart manifesting itself by generousity,"[9] and *kardia* which means "the heart; the vigor and sense of physical life, the center and seat of spiritual life."[10]

- **Wholeheartedly:** From the Greek word *eunoia* which means "good will, kindness."[11]

- **Threaten:** From the Greek word *apeile* which means "a threatening, threat."[12]

- **Favoritism:** From the Greek word *prosopolepsia* which means "respect of persons; partiality."[13]

- **Armor of God:** From two Greek words: *panoplia* which means "full armour, complete armour,"[14] and *theos* which means "a god or goddess, a general name of deities or divinities; the Godhead; spoken of the only and true God; whatever can in any respect be likened unto God, or resemble Him in any way."[15]

- **Struggle:** From the Greek word *pale* which means "wrestling (a contest between two in which each endeavours to throw the other, and which is decided when the victor is able to hold his opponent down with his hand upon his neck)."[16]

- **Flesh:** From the Greek word *sarx* which means "flesh (the soft substance of the living body, which covers the bones and is permeated with blood) of both man and beasts; the body; a living creature (because possessed of a body of flesh) whether man or beast; the flesh, denotes mere human nature, the earthly nature of man apart from divine influence, and therefore prone to sin and opposed to God."[17]

- **Blood:** From the Greek word *haima* which means "blood; blood shed, to be shed by violence, slay, murder."[18]

- **Rulers:** From the Greek word *arche* which means "beginning, origin; the person or thing that commences, the first person or thing in a series, the leader; that by which anything begins to be, the origin, the active cause; the extremity of a thing; the first place, principality, rule, magistracy."[19]

- **Authorities:** From the Greek word *kosmokrator* which means "lord of the world, prince of this age."[20]

- **Powers:** From the Greek word *exousia* which means "power of choice, liberty of doing as one pleases; physical and mental power; the power of authority (influence) and of right (privilege); the power of rule or government (the power of him whose will and commands must be submitted to by others and obeyed)."[21]

- **Forces:** From the Greek word *poneria* which means "depravity, iniquity, wickedness; malice; evil purposes and desires."[22]

- **Belt of truth:** From three Greek words: *osphus* which means "the hip (loin), to gird, gird about, the loins; a loin, the (two) loins,"[23] *perizonnumi* which means "to fasten garments with a girdle or bel; to gird one's self; metaph. with truth as a girdle,"[24] and *aletheia* which means "objectively what is true in any matter under consideration, what is true in things appertaining to God and the duties of man, moral and religious truth, the truth as taught in the Christian religion, respecting God and the execution of his purposes through Christ, and respecting the duties of man, opposing alike to the superstitions of the Gentiles and the inventions of the Jews, and the corrupt opinions and precepts of false teachers even among Christians; subjectively truth as a personal excellence."[25]

- **Breastplate of righteousness:** From two Greek words: *thorax* which means "the breast, the part of the body from the neck to the navel, where the ribs end; a breastplate or corset consisting of two parts and protecting the body on both sides from the neck to the middle,"[26] and *dikaiosune* which means "in a broad sense: state of him who is as he ought to be, righteousness, the condition acceptable to God; in a narrower sense, justice or the virtue which gives each his due."[27]

- **Feet fitted with readiness:** From three Greek words: *pous* which means "a foot, both of men or beast,"[28] *hupodeo* which means "to underbind; to bind under one's self, bind on,"[29] and *hetoimasia* which means "the act of preparing; the condition of a person or thing so far forth as prepared, preparedness, readiness."[30]

- **Shield of faith:** From two Greek words: *thureos* which means "a shield, a large oblong, four cornered shield,"[31] and *pistis* which means "conviction of the truth of anything, belief; in the

NT of a conviction or belief respecting man's relationship to God and divine things, generally with the included idea of trust and holy fervor born of faith and joined with it; fidelity, faithfulness."[32]

- **Flaming arrows:** From two Greek words: *puro* which means "to burn with fire, to set on fire, kindle"[33] and *belos* which means "a missile, dart, javelin, arrow."[34]

- **Helmet of salvation:** From two Greek words: *perikephalaia* which means "a helmet; metaph. the protection of the soul which consists in (the hope of) salvation,"[35] and *soterion* which means "saving, bringing salvation; he who embodies this salvation, or through whom God is about to achieve it; the hope of (future) salvation."[36]

- **Sword of the Spirit:** From two Greek words: *machaira* which means "a large knife, used for killing animals and cutting up flesh; a small sword, as distinguished from a large sword,"[37] and *pneuma* which means "a movement of air (a gentle blast) of the wind, hence the wind itself, breath of nostrils or mouth; the spirit, i.e. the vital principal by which the body is animated; a spirit, i.e. a simple essence, devoid of all or at least all grosser matter, and possessed of the power of knowing, desiring, deciding, and acting; of God; the disposition or influence which fills and governs the soul of any one."[38]

- **Pray:** From the Greek word *proseuchomai* which means "to offer prayers, to pray."[39]

- **Alert:** From the Greek word *agrupneo* which means "to be sleepless, keep awake, watch; to be circumspect, attentive, ready."[40]

- **Tychicus:** From the Greek word *Tuchikos* which means "Tychicus = "fateful." an Asiatic Christian, friend and companion of the apostle Paul."[41]

- **Encourage:** From the Greek word *parakaleo* which means "to call to one's side, call for, summon; to address, speak to, (call to, call upon), which may be done in the way of exhortation, entreaty, comfort, instruction, etc."[42]

- **Undying:** From the Greek word *aphtharsia* which means "incorruption, perpetuity; purity, sincerity, incorrupt."[43]

Ephesians 6:1-4

Children, obey your parents in the Lord, for this is right. "Honor your father and mother" – which is the first commandment with a promise – "that it may go well with you and that you may enjoy long life on the earth."

Fathers, do not exasperate your children; instead, bring them up in the training and instruction of the Lord.

(Related Bible references: Exodus 20:12, Deuteronomy 4:9, Deuteronomy 5:16, Deuteronomy 6:7, Proverbs 1:8, Proverbs 3:11, Proverbs 6:20, Proverbs 13:24, Proverbs 19:18, Proverbs 20:20, Proverbs 22:1, Proverbs 22:6, Proverbs 23:22, Proverbs 24:21, Matthew 15:4, Mark 10:13-16, John 17:5-23, Colossians 3:20-21, 1 Timothy 5:3, Hebrews 12:9, 1 Peter 2:17)

Jesus told His followers that He was leaving them in the world, not to be of it, but to remain in it (John 17:5-23). These controversial words have led to all sorts of different beliefs, ideas, and concepts about just what it means to be in the world, but not of it. This is to be understood, if for no other reason, that the world is a big place, with many differing ideas on how to accomplish things. Some people believe that being in the world but not of it means that Christians should live among themselves, isolated. Some believe it means avoiding the latest technology or social trends. Others think that it means the Christian should spend extensive time alone. Whether the way the idea manifests in dress, in approach to social custom, language, hairstyles, or anything else, it seems as if it's obvious that Christians throughout the ages have tried very hard to manage the balance of living in the world, without being of it, in many ways.

Down to the present age, there's an air in the church that says, "We know it all!" We think low of the answers that people have had to past solutions, and we scoff at anyone or anything who sees things differently. We have mastered, in the modern church, the art of being in the world, but not the part where we are not supposed to be so glaringly a part of it. We've adapted little parts here and there, rejecting any hint that maybe modern technology, modern pushes for money and wealth, or the things that we generally pursue are the wrong priorities. We have deluded ourselves that the way to attract the world is to have what the world has, be how the world is, and sound just like the world sounds. We have, on a large scale, become highly ineffective in our witness and in the way that we respond to others, to their needs and the concerns that this world has. Somewhere in here, I think that we have lost sight of Jesus' words to us, and the purpose of the church in the world. We have taken up causes and stopped being effective, stopped being exactly the things that we are supposed to be.

That's why Ephesians is such an important book, especially considering exactly what we, as a church, should be doing while we are here and what we should be doing as individual people. We have lost sight of our eternal positioning and purpose, our proper leadership, our proper beliefs, and our proper view of relationships. We don't know who we are, and we often don't know where we are going.

Identity is essential to church membership and participation. We need to recognize our purpose in this world. We need to see ourselves, valuable in Christ, with a contribution to bring to the table. So when someone attempts to teach on part of Ephesians 6 without considering the rest of the book and its contents, it's not a surprise that much of it doesn't make sense. It takes on another character, one that is almost unreasonably aggressive, when it comes to a spiritual response to the things we will encounter in this world.

Ephesians chapter 6 addresses worldly issues: parenting, slavery, spiritual warfare, and doing the work of ministry. It provides for us answers to many of the hostilities we encounter but does so with a certain grace and balance that we don't hear when we embrace teaching on these topics. The book of Ephesians is amazingly balanced when discussing practical matters, always providing a counterbalance for every position listed. The Apostle Paul doesn't just talk to wives, he also talks to husbands; he doesn't just talk to children, he also talks to parents; he doesn't just talk to slaves, he also talks to masters. This equalizing measure exists to remind us that nobody is any better than anybody else, and that when we are in relationships, we are still accountable for ourselves. If we want to be people of authority, we must recognize the relevance in mastering ourselves. The values of the world are going to be different than ours, and this means that we will encounter differences of opinions with other people (sometimes in our closest relationships). This means that we must measure and account for how we both behave and treat others – and must aware ourselves of how we are in every situation of our lives.

The Apostle Paul opens chapter 6 by advising

children to obey their parents, because it is right, and obeying parents is the first commandment given with a promise, because such will lead to a long life in the land. By obedience, children reflect respect for their parents, and respect goes a long way in life, as we can see in many places within the Scriptures:

Being respected [A good name/reputation] is more important than having great riches. To be well thought of [High esteem] is better than silver or gold [Eccl. 7:1]. (Proverbs 22:1, EXB)

My child [son], respect [fear] the Lord and the king. Don't join those people who refuse to obey them [rebel]. (Proverbs 24:21, EXB)

Take care of [Provide support for; or Honor; Show respect to; both honor and financial help are likely in mind] widows who are truly widows. (1 Timothy 5:3, EXB)

[Furthermore; Moreover] We have all had fathers [or parents] here on earth who disciplined us, and we respected them. So it is even more important that we accept discipline from the Father of our spirits [or our spiritual Father; or the Father of all spirit beings; 12:23; Num. 16:22] so we will have [eternal or true spiritual] life. (Hebrews 12:9, EXB)

Show respect for [Honor] all people: Love the brothers and sisters of God's family [community of believers; brotherhood], respect [fear] God [Prov. 1:7], honor the king [or emperor; Rom. 13:1]. (1 Peter 2:17, EXB)

This passage continues commentary on the Roman Codes, a carryover from Chapter 5. Under the Roman Codes, fathers had the legal right to treat their children any way they desired, even unto disowning them for any reason. The Apostle Paul starts by issuing important principles of respect, especially in context of respecting parents. He then reminds parents they have responsibilities toward their children. Over-discipline is as bad as under-discipline, and ultimately, parents are accountable before God for the way they treat their children.

Respect gives us the ability to interact with other people in a manner that acknowledges personal boundaries and both earthly and God-given authority. It starts young, as we can see here, in this passage. Respect is something taught, as adults enforce the principle that children should show respect to those who are older and responsible for their well-being. It is also something that extends far beyond the concept of just biological or natural parents. Obeying and honoring parents relates to honoring our ancestors, those who have made it possible to be where we are in life, and who have taught us, down the ages, having received instruction at some point, directly from our divine source. Respecting authority means we respect what they have worked for, we respect the land, and we respect the sacrifices that have been made to make sure we can have the best possible, down to today.

This passage also relates to spiritual authority: to those who are our spiritual parents and leaders, those who seek our best interests at heart, and who guide us in love, not in control. There are many, many good leaders in this world who guide the people God has assigned to them properly, walking in the offices God has appointed them to serve in, and who care about training people to live proper Christian lives and the grace of submitting one to another.

In parenthood, parents are also told to avoid exasperating their children. In other words, the Bible tells us that parents should not abuse their children, and that child abuse is wrong. I acknowledge that we don't all agree on exactly where the lines are between discipline and abuse, but it's also clear that we have spent so much time trying to argue those lines and move them here and there according to our own egotistical arguments that we've forgotten our disagreements are not important. Discipline of children should not be about what we want to do to our children, but about what God expects us to do with our children. The job of parenthood is to focus on the socialization of our children or helping children to develop the necessary skills to survive in the world and interact properly in society. Being a father, a mother, or a caregiver to a child is about developing that child, not about using the children for an adult's purposes. This is true with anger, it is true with sexual expressions, and it is true with emotional outbursts. If they are rightly grounded, they will live long in the land and will live lives that reflect success at what they choose to do.

In keeping with these realities, Christian parents are not just raising their children to fit in with society, but also, to be future adults within the Kingdom of God. In raising children right, not being exceedingly harsh but remembering the importance of balanced discipline, seeing to their educational and social needs, and working to raise children in a responsible way, parents should also see to the spiritual needs of their children. Children need to hear the instruction and training of the Lord, so that it can carry them through life. Proverbs 22:6 says:

Train children to live the right way [in their/or his path; referring either to children or to God], and when they are old, they will not stray [depart] from it. (EXB)

The passage promises that once children reach a point of balance in their lives, they will not depart from the truths they have been taught. It is why, speaking of children, Mark 10:13-16 says:

Some people brought their little children to Jesus so He could touch them, but His followers [disciples] told them to stop [scolded/rebuked them]. When Jesus saw this, He was upset [angry; indignant] and said to them, "Let the little children come to Me. Don't stop them, because the Kingdom of God belongs to people who are like these children [meaning humble and dependent]. I tell you the truth, you must accept the Kingdom of God as if you were a little child, or you will never enter it." Then Jesus took the children in His arms, put [laid] His hands on them, and blessed them. (EXB)

Children are a part of the church, too, no questions asked. Children should be welcome at church, at Sunday school, and in different activities or church involvements. This means that every Christian family should see to it that they are a part of a church that has appropriate education and programs for children of differing ages. With the right church support, children and families can also have the right support, in practical ways and with a spiritual community rather than just a secular support group that builds up commonalities rather than edification.

Ephesians 6:5-9

Slaves, obey your earthly masters with respect and fear, and with sincerity of heart, just as you would obey Christ. Obey them not only to win their favor when their eye is on you, but like slaves of Christ, doing the will of God from your heart. Serve wholeheartedly, as if you were serving the Lord, not men, because you know that the Lord will reward everyone for whatever good he does, whether he is slave or free.

And masters, treat your slaves in the same way. Do not threaten them, since you know that He Who is both their Master and yours is in heaven, and there is no favoritism with Him.

(Related Bible references: Leviticus 25:43, 1 Corinthians 7:22, Galatians 3:28, Colossians 3:22-24, 1 Timothy 6:1, 1 Peter 2:18, Revelation 18:11-14)

Many people, especially social activists, take issue with the way the Bible refers to slavery. This is because they understand it in a more modern context, which is radically different from the Biblical context of slavery. It has also not helped that many slavery advocates attempt to use Biblical passages that refer to slavery, as if it somehow justifies their position.

I do not believe that the enslavement of human beings by other human beings was ever a part of God's intention or purpose for us. Slavery is something that is specifically mentioned as being overthrown and overturned with the fall of Babylon, thus making it something that is a part of the world, found in Revelation 18:11-14:

And the merchants of the earth will cry [weep] and be sad about her, because now there is no one to buy their cargoes— cargoes of gold, silver, jewels [precious stones], pearls, fine linen, purple cloth, silk, red [scarlet] cloth; all kinds of citron wood and all kinds of things made from ivory, expensive wood, bronze, iron, and marble; [and cargoes of] cinnamon, spice, incense, myrrh, frankincense, wine, olive oil, fine flour, wheat, cattle, sheep, horses, carriages [wagons], slaves, and human lives [bodies and human souls].

The merchants will say [implied by the context],

"Babylon, the good things [fruit] you wanted [desired; longed for] are gone from you.
All your rich [expensive; luxurious] and fancy [glamorous; shining] things have disappeared.
You will never have [find] them again." (EXB)

If slavery is a part of the world, that means it is something that should not be practiced by the church, period, in any of its forms. If this is the case, then why is it mentioned at all in the Bible? The reason is simpler than we might want to consider, and in all our attempts to be super-deep, we are missing the obvious. Slavery is mentioned in the Bible, and at least on the surface, somewhat tolerated, because it was a part of the economic culture of society at the time. When the church started, there were slaves, and slaves who wanted to join the church. There were also slave owners who wanted to join the church and had slaves. Because there were legal and economic reasons why slavery existed, the Bible addressed a common issue of the time, that was a part of the social world of the first century. It was not in any way comparable to more modern forms of slavery (including that which was done in European and American history as a foundation for modern-day racism), which I will not be examining here, because it does not have a Biblical foundation, in the least.

Slavery, as was noted in ancient cultures, is something that emerged for four purposes. The first was for debt repayment. People were commonly enslaved in ancient times because they owed out a large sum of money to someone else and were unable to pay it back. As a result, slavery in this context related largely to many principles that we find in Christianity – keeping one's word, keeping one's commitment, and honoring debts – all related to slavery for the reason of debt repayment. The other three reasons for slavery were less economic: one was slavery as a result of wartime, as people were acquired prisoners of war, or war criminals; some were prisoners, working out crimes committed in society (such as theft or damage to property); and some people were slaves, due to inheritance (a master died and left his slaves to his children or family).

There are many reasons why slaves would have been attracted to Christianity. In the ancient world of religion, slavery was regarded as a punishment because someone had done something to displease God. This was not so in Christianity, where slaves were given the same status and opportunity to repent and change before God as anyone else. In Christ, slaves were free, but that didn't mean that the economic and political systems of their day recognized their new-found spiritual freedom. How, now, could a slave experience freedom in Christ when they were still enslaved by the world?

The Apostle Paul's perspective was to encourage slaves to behave as they would in any other situation. He calls them to be respectful, to do the work that is assigned to them, and do so with a good attitude, remembering that the One we who are in Christ all serve was watching, and He gives recompense. Instead of ignoring or revolting against their economic and legal responsibilities, they were encouraged to repay their debt, their obligation, or their service, with Christ in mind.

Modern interpretations of this passage tend to speak of employees and employers, although the analogy doesn't fit in the exact same way. There are precepts here that can relate to being a good employee, however, and things that we should keep in mind when we are in situations where we owe a debt, of sorts, to someone else. If we owe a debt, we need to repay it by any means necessary. We should not be comfortable with not paying our bills, not taking care of responsibilities, and not doing right by other people. Anyone who is employed should do their job wholeheartedly, with sincerity of heart, and the importance of doing what is right on a job. God rewards all, and God is still above anyone who has rule over someone else. When we have the right character, even in a situation where we feel like we have gotten a raw deal, God still calls us to do the right thing.

On the other hand, those who were masters of slaves were told to treat slaves in the same way that slaves were to treat them! Rather than being about getting something out of them, masters were encouraged to be kind and Christian with their slaves. They were to treat them as brothers and sisters in the Lord, kindly, and without abuse. They were not to be threatening, and to always recall that there was no favoritism with God.

Abusing other people because you can is something that isn't going to fly in view of eternity.

If we are to talk about those who are owed a debt as well as employers, there is something important here to consider. Forgiveness goes a long way, and earthly authority is empty if God is not in it. While employees and masters with slaves had earthly authority, that doesn't mean they had or have it in the light of eternity. When someone is given a position of authority, it must be used wisely, and in a certain level of balance. It's fine to have a leadership or authority role, but not if it is being used for puffing up or arrogance. God, Who sees all, does have a way of leveling things out, and all of us should be mindful of ourselves, whenever we feel that we are in a position that is higher than someone else's.

Ephesians 6:10-20

Finally, be strong in the Lord and in His mighty power. Put on the full armor of God so that you can take your stand against the devil's schemes. For our struggle is not against flesh and blood, but against the rulers, against the authorities, against the powers of this dark world and against the spiritual forces of evil in the heavenly realms. Therefore put on the full armor of God, so that when the evil day comes, you may be able to stand your ground, and after you have done everything, to stand. Stand firm then, with the belt of truth buckled around your waist, with the breastplate of righteousness in place, and with your feet fitted with the readiness that comes from the Gospel of peace. In addition to all this, take up the shield of faith, with which you can extinguish all the flaming arrows of the evil one. Take the helmet of salvation and the sword of the Spirit, which is the Word of God. And pray in the Spirit on all occasions with all kinds of prayers and requests. With this in mind, be alert and always keep on

praying for all the saints.

Pray also for me, that whenever I open my mouth, words may be given me so that I will fearlessly make known the mystery of the Gospel, for which I am an ambassador in chains. Pray that I may declare it fearlessly, as I should.

(Related Bible references: Psalm 37:4, Proverbs 4:23, Job 32:8, Job 33:4, Isaiah 11:5, Isaiah 52:7, Isaiah 59:17, Acts 10:36, Romans 8:26-27, Romans 10:15, 1 Corinthians 16:13, 2 Corinthians 3:2, 2 Corinthians 4:16, 2 Corinthians 5:20, 2 Corinthians 6:7, 2 Corinthians 10:5, Colossians 2:7, Colossians 4:2-4, 1 Thessalonians 5:8, Hebrews 4:12, Jude 1:20)

If there's one topic that seems to be on everyone's minds these days, it is spiritual warfare. It seems as if every time you turn around, go on the internet, or go in a Christian bookstore, there is another book designed to calm every concern or fear you have with some sort of spiritual prayer or methodical approach. It has been my own experience that many of these books and teachings induce a certain sense of paranoia into someone's life. All of a sudden, everything becomes a result of spiritual warfare. Have a headache? Someone is working witchcraft against you! Stub your toe? Someone wished you dead! Did your child fall off their bike? Someone wants your ministry and your family to be gone!

I used to assume people were not so gullible to fall for this type of thinking in every single instance...but I have found myself to be very, very wrong in that assumption. We live in a world where we don't want to be accountable, and simple explanations of things are often overlooked in favor of more dramatic, spiritual ones. People who are in church and don't want to see a practical solution to a situation (maybe you have allergies, or maybe you should pay more attention to where you are walking, or maybe your child isn't experienced with bike riding yet) are apt to jump on the bandwagon and start using what they perceive to be spiritual answers to everyday problems.

The catch with the way we are approaching spiritual warfare is that it isn't changing the everyday, ordinary encounters we have that are not spiritual in nature. People can get headaches, stub their toes, and kids fall off bikes for completely non-spiritually related reasons. The nature of the flesh means that sometimes people do things for completely personal reasons that have nothing to do with either the enemy or God, and we must take all this into consideration when considering the realm of spiritual warfare. The fact that these methods are so ineffective turns people indifferent to the true spiritual enemies and realities that we must face, and the true reasons for spiritual warfare. Even though the modern-day church has made spiritual warfare a fanciful, almost laughable demon-chasing activity, Christians do have a real enemy, we have people in this lifetime who reflect this enemy, thus manifesting in the natural as our enemies, and we are confronted, every day, with these different realities. This means we, as Christians, need to know how best to handle it.

The first piece of advice is to remain strong in the Lord, and His power. We most effectively do this by remaining connected to Him and living and loving as He commands us to do. There is something to be said for remaining peaceful in adversity and remaining stable in difficult situations. While the world gets upset, remaining peaceful and balanced is always a line of defense. Being strong doesn't mean being aggressive; it means being able to bear and withstand whatever comes along, without being easily burdened or flinched.

It's been said that the best defense is also the best offense. This can be applied to the principle of spiritual armor, which we are commanded to put on as believers. Nothing mentioned in this passage encourages believers to be hostile or aggressive, but to use that which is available to them spiritually. The reason we are encouraged to do this is for one reason, and one reason only: the devil is a schemer, and the different powers, principalities, authorities, and spiritual forces have a way of working for him, tipping the scales in his favor. The enemy will use whoever he desires, whenever it is convenient, even those we might not expect or consider, in order to keep us easily distracted. If we recognize that some of the things that happen to us (especially when dealing with the world and the powers of this world) because the enemy is trying to get at us by using other people and spiritual forces, then we can step up and defend ourselves, spiritually prepared and ready to stand when issues come up. We are called to do everything that we can do, and when we have done that, still stand. When we've done what makes sense, what doesn't make sense, what seems the most spiritual, what seems the most rational, and nothing has worked, we can still stand, because we are ready and prepared for whatever might come against us. We are to stand firm with:

- **Belt of truth buckled around the waist:** It shouldn't come as much of a surprise that the spiritual armor mentioned here is parallel in appearance to the natural armor worn by military personnel in the first century. Armor was a protective point, and spiritual armor serves that same point. The belt of truth buckled around the waist holds us up, as truth does in our lives. If we are buckled with truth, which keeps our pants or skirt up, our shirt tucked in, and our appearance together, then we can stand firm and upright, without shame or embarrassment.

- **Breastplate of righteousness in place:** The breastplate protects the chest area, particularly the innards of the heart, lungs, and other essential internal organs. If we allow righteousness to guard our heart, we will follow the ways of the Lord and He will give us the desires of our heart (Psalm 37:4). If we allow righteousness to protect our lungs, we will breathe in the breath of the Spirit with every breath (Job 32:8, Job 33:4). If we allow righteousness to protect our most delicate inwardness, then we will be guided and directed by God, even in our most intimate thoughts, moments, and issues (2 Corinthians 4:16).

It's also relevant to say the breastplate must be "in place." Placing it incorrectly could be as bad as not wearing it at all. Making sure righteousness is in position in our lives is paramount to living as spiritual people in a difficult world.

- **Feet fitted with the readiness that comes from the Gospel of peace:** We should be the first to move with the Spirit as He guides us, moving in peace rather than hostility or anger, and good judgment rather than impulsivity. God has given us the right preparation, and as we exercise our preparation, we are ready for our walk with God, our calling, and to answer our greater life purpose. Movement in peace is a lifestyle that we are properly fitted for, something that fits us right and has us ready for every moment that we will encounter in this life.

- **Shield of faith, which extinguishes flaming arrows:** The enemy doesn't play fair; that's why he is the enemy, and why he has his victories. He has a way of hitting us where it hurts most, alluring us with what we want the most to get us away from where we need to be, and attacking us right at the time we need it least. Given this, the shield of faith, which is held slightly out in front of the body, is there to extinguish these flaming arrows. Flaming arrows, or arrows lit on fire and then shot at an opposing force, were a primary weapon of defense (not to mention a rather effective one) that required the opposing force to somehow extinguish them and prevent them from entering the body. A shield was effective for this, as is the shield of faith. If our faith is our first defense, it means that our trust and confidence in God is the first thing we should have around us, keeping things from invading our being. When the enemy comes at us with his best shot, our continued faith and perseverance to God's plan for us is the best defense to put down anything Satan wants to send our way to take us out.

- **Helmet of salvation:** Helmets protect heads from injuries. This is important, as our head contains our brain, which controls the functions of our entire body. The helmet of salvation reminds us that it is important to protect what goes into our head – our thoughts, processes, images, ideas, concepts, and other similar things – which might easily cause us to derail off course.

- **Sword of the Spirit, which is the Word of God:** We learn in Hebrews 4:12 that:

  God's Word is living and active. It is sharper than any two-edged sword and cuts as deep as the place where soul and spirit meet, the place where joints and marrow meet. God's Word judges a person's thoughts and intentions. (GW)

  The word, "word" is the Greek word, *rhema*, which refers to any spoken word that comes (in this instance) from God. The sword of the Spirit as the word of God is the proper use of Scripture and relaying God's words to us in our lives, recognizing the benefit of both as a powerful weapon against the work of the enemy. If we are understanding of Scripture in our lives and of forma of spoken revelation (word of knowledge, word of wisdom, and prophecy), we will know what God is doing in season and out of season. There is power in speaking the right words at the right time – not for the sake of getting what we want, but because word in due season is essential.

- **Pray in the Spirit on all occasions, with many kinds of prayers:** Praying in the Spirit is more than just speaking in tongues, although that is definitely a part of it. To pray in the Spirit means to be in touch with the intercession of the Spirit (Romans 8:26-27), knowing what to pray for and when. There are many ways we can pray, and we are encouraged to familiarize ourselves with many kinds of prayers, so we are ready to pray in all situations and communicate exactly what we desire to communicate to God, no matter what the situation may be.

- **Be alert and keep praying for the saints:** Being alert means being watchful and prepared. In a state of alertness, we aren't falling asleep on the job, ignoring the things that are going on around us, nor the things that are going on in the spiritual realm. It doesn't mean becoming a miracle chaser, nor a demon chaser, but finding the middle ground between awareness and obsession with things that lead us away from where we should be. Not only should we be aware, but we should be thinking of others in the body, praying for the saints: for those we know and those we don't know, our leaders and our friends, our brothers and sisters in Christ, our missionaries and all who are a part of this family of faith, the church, that is walking with God in our day and age.

None of these things listed as a part of spiritual warfare involve fancy exorcisms, spitting, screaming, throwing water or oil at people, running around in circles, begging other people to help us, running to our neighbors for protection, being present with a camera to record the whole incident, or vanishing to hide. The armor of the Lord says nothing about covering our backsides, which means that they shouldn't be left to be vulnerable and exposed. No, we are given the ability to stand; to be spiritually aware; and to be prepared in each situation. God does not tell us to avoid the battle, but to be ready for it, and to expect that it will come at different times of our lives.

The Apostle Paul closes this section by asking for prayer for himself: that he might fearlessly proclaim the Gospel, and move in faith, as he should. This reminds us of how important prayer is for our leaders, those who have personally deposited into our lives, and those who benefit from that deposit, indirectly. The Apostle Paul is not the personal apostle of any living person today, because he lived so long ago. We are still reading his words, however, and gaining a greater insight into what God asks of us today because of the impact he had on the churches of the first century. Even though you may not directly know an apostle, you know someone whose life is being transformed or changed by one. Remember leaders in prayer, even those you do not personally know. It is a difficult task to be in leadership, and to constantly come up against the world. The hostilities and warfare that leaders face is intense, and it is through prayer and encouragement that leaders (especially apostles) can endure and overcome.

Ephesians 6:21-24

Tychicus, the dear brother and faithful servant in the Lord, will tell you everything, so that you also may know how I am and what I am doing. I am sending him to you for this very purpose, that you may know how we are, and that he may encourage you.

Peace to the brothers, and love with faith from God the Father and the Lord Jesus Christ. Grace to all who love our Lord Jesus Christ with an undying love.

(Related Bible references: Matthew 16:18, Acts 20:4, Colossians 4:7-8, Colossians 4:18, 2 Timothy 4:12, Titus 3:12)

Tychicus is not a name that immediately comes to mind when we think of New Testament characters. He is one of several diverse people that the Apostle Paul mentions in his different letters who was of help to him in some way. From what we know of history, Tychicus accompanied the Apostle Paul on at least part of one of his journeys and was in contact with the apostle while in Rome. Tychius is mentioned five times in the New Testament, the four outside of Ephesians can be found here:

Sopater (son of Pyrrhus) from Berea, Aristarchus and Secundus from Thessalonica, Gaius from Derbe, Timothy, and Tychicus and Trophimus from the province of Asia accompanied Paul. (Acts 20:4, GW)

I'm sending Tychicus to you. He is our dear brother, trustworthy deacon, and partner in the Lord's work. He will tell you everything that is happening to me. (Colossians 4:7, GW)

I'm sending Tychicus to the city of Ephesus as my representative. (2 Timothy 4:12, GW)

When I send Artemas or Tychicus to you, hurry to visit me in the city of Nicopolis. I have decided to spend the winter there. (Titus 3:2, GW)

Tychius is here to remind all of us how important faithfulness and service are before God. Leaders cannot be everywhere all the time, and the Kingdom requires faithful individuals who can be trusted with a message, a task, or a responsibility. Encouragement comes in many forms, and while we are quick to think that verbal praise or acknowledgement is important to a leader, there are many other ways that we can encourage those who labor among us. Faithfulness, reliability, accountability, and dedicated service are all an encouragement to a leader, especially if they exemplify those same attributes in themselves. If we want to please not only our spiritual leaders but God as well, we need to pass from a place where we only verbally acknowledge people and start showing others that a change has occurred within us. We cannot expect praise if we do not exemplify progress, and we cannot exemplify progress if we have not put into practice what is expected of each of us.

Much as in his opening, the Apostle Paul closes with peace, love, and grace. Those three words have been a consistent theme throughout Ephesians, which means they must be a consistent theme flowing through the church. Through Christ, we have experienced God's love. Through grace, we have experienced salvation. Through the working of our faith, we come to a place where we experience peace. The church that has existed since the beginning is within us now, working and changing us from the inside out. We are a part of it, and she is a part of us. Called from sin and darkness, we are here in a place where we can receive the grace of God and experience Him in our lives.

No matter how bleak it may look as people give the church a bad name, never forget Jesus' promise in Matthew 16:18:

So I tell you, you are Peter [the Greek petros, like the Aramaic cephas, means "rock" or "stone"]. On this rock I will build my church, and the power of death [gates of Hades/the underworld] will not be able to defeat [overpower; conquer; prevail against] it. (EXB)

The church just isn't big-name preachers or lost congregants. It isn't just people who claim to be

Christian but really are not. It's not just big denominations, or wayward clergy, or scholars who think they know everything about the Bible, but do not. The church is you and me, and the church is worth fighting for, defending, and embracing. If the church shall withstand the gates of hell, no matter what hell throws at her, then we, too shall stand on the side of life and shall endure. We can make it to the end of this battle. God hasn't given up on us, and we shouldn't give up on Him, or on His church. If we are here, as long as we are breathing, as long as we have life, we can walk in those gifts and promises that can be found only in the church. The church reminds us that life is bigger than us, and life is eternal...and that in eternal life, we find a different purpose for ourselves and our perspective of it all. In one singular word, this difference, simply put, is love.

References

[1](https://www.google.com/search?client=firefox-b-1-d&q=maverick+city+build+your+church+lyrics&sei=Hmp6aOaZBML9kPIPtr3DgAY). Accessed July 18, 2025

Introduction

- "Ephesus." https://en.wikipedia.org/wiki/Ephesus. Accessed December 10, 2015.
- "Epistle To The Ephesians." https://en.wikipedia.org/wiki/Epistle_to_the_Ephesians. Accessed December 10, 2015.
- "Paul the Apostle." https://en.wikipedia.org/wiki/Paul_the_Apostle. Accessed December 10, 2015.

Chapter 1

[1] Strong's Exhaustive Concordance of the Bible, #3972
[2] Ibid., #2307
[3] Ibid., #40
[4] Ibid., #2181
[5] Ibid, #4103
[6] Ibid., #5485
[7] Ibid., #1515
[8] Ibid., #2128
[9] Ibid., #2127
[10] Ibid., #2032
[11] Ibid., #1586
[12] Ibid., #4253
[13] Ibid., #2602
[14] Ibid., #2889
[15] Ibid., #40
[16] Ibid., #299
[17] Ibid., #26
[18] Ibid., #4309

[19] Ibid., #5206
[20] Ibid., #629
[21] Ibid., #859
[22] Ibid., #4149
[23] Ibid., #4678
[24] Ibid., #5428
[25] Ibid., #4138
[26] Ibid., #2098
[27] Ibid., #4991
[28] Ibid., #2817
[29] Ibid., #4102
[30] Ibid., #5461
[31] Ibid., #1680
[32] Ibid., #2479

Chapter 2

[1] Strong's Exhaustive Concordance of the Bible, #3498
[2] Ibid., #3900
[3] Ibid., #266
[4] Ibid., #758
[5] Ibid., #1849
[6] Ibid., #165
[7] Ibid., #543
[8] Ibid., #4561
[9] Ibid., #5043
[10] Ibid., #3709
[11] Ibid., #1656
[12] Ibid., 4806
[13] Ibid., #4982
[14] Ibid., #5544
[15] Ibid., #2041
[16] Ibid., #2744
[17] Ibid., #4161
[18] Ibid., #1484
[19] Ibid., #203
[20] Ibid., #4061
[21] Ibid., #526
[22] Ibid., #3112
[23] Ibid., #1451
[24] Ibid., #3320
[25] Ibid., #5418
[26] Ibid., #2673
[27] Ibid., #1785
[28] Ibid., #1378
[29] Ibid., #604
[30] Ibid., #4318
[31] Ibid., #3581
[32] Ibid., #3941
[33] Ibid., #4847
[34] Ibid., #3609
[35] Ibid., #2310

[36] Ibid., #204
[37] Ibid., #3485
[38] Ibid., #2732

Chapter 3

[1] Strong's Exhaustive Concordance of the Bible, #1198
[2] Ibid., #3622
[3] Ibid., #3466
[4] Ibid., #602
[5] Ibid., #1074
[6] Ibid., #4789
[7] Ibid., #613
[8] Ibid., #746
[9] Ibid., #1849
[10] Ibid., #4286
[11] Ibid., #3954
[12] Ibid., 4006
[13] Ibid., #1573
[14] Ibid., #1119
[15] Ibid., #3965
[16] Ibid., #2901
[17] Ibid., #5228

Chapter 4

[1] Strong's Exhaustive Concordance of the Bible, #516
[2] Ibid., #5012
[3] Ibid., #4236
[4] Ibid., #3115
[5] Ibid., #1775
[6] Ibid., #1520
[7] Ibid., #2821
[8] Ibid., #908
[9] Ibid., #1390
[10] Ibid., #652
[11] Ibid., #4396
[12] Ibid., 2099
[13] Ibid., #4166
[14] Ibid., #1320
[15] Ibid., #1248
[16] Ibid., #5046
[17] Ibid., #3516
[18] Ibid., #2831
[19] Ibid., #2940
[20] Ibid., #3834
[21] Ibid., #4106
[22] Ibid., #837
[23] Ibid., #2776
[24] Ibid., #860
[25] Ibid., #5579
[26] Ibid., #225

[27] Ibid., #4139
[28] Ibid., #3710
[29] Ibid., #5117
[30] Ibid., #2813
[31] Ibid., #4550
[32] Ibid., #3056
[33] Ibid., #3076
[34] Ibid., #4972
[35] Ibid., #4088
[36] Ibid., #2372
[37] Ibid., #2549
[38] Ibid., #988
[39] Ibid., #2155

Chapter 5

[1] Strong's Exhaustive Concordance of the Bible, #3402
[2] Ibid., #4376
[3] Ibid., #2175
[4] Ibid., #2378
[5] Author's explanatory note
[6] Strong's Exhaustive Concordance of the Bible, #4202
[7] Ibid., #167
[8] Ibid., #4124
[9] Ibid., #151
[10] Ibid., #3473
[11] Ibid., #2160
[12] Ibid., 2169
[13] Ibid., #1496
[14] Ibid., #175
[15] Ibid., #2041
[16] Ibid., #4655
[17] Ibid., #1651
[18] Ibid., #3182
[19] Ibid., #3631
[20] Ibid., #4137
[21] Ibid., #5568
[22] Ibid., #5215
[23] Ibid., #4152
[24] Ibid., #5603
[25] Ibid., #103
[26] Ibid., #5567
[27] Ibid., #5293
[28] Ibid., #1135
[29] Ibid., #2776
[30] Ibid., #435
[31] Ibid., #3860
[32] Ibid., #1438
[33] Ibid., #37
[34] Ibid., #5204
[35] Ibid., #4487
[36] Ibid., #1741

[37] Ibid., #4696
[38] Ibid., #4512
[39] Ibid., #299
[40] Ibid., #4983
[41] Ibid., #3173
[42] Ibid., #5399

Chapter 6

[1] Strong's Exhaustive Concordance of the Bible, #5043
[2] Ibid., #5219
[3] Ibid., #1118
[4] Ibid., #1342
[5] Ibid., #3962
[6] Ibid., #3949
[7] Ibid., #1401
[8] Ibid., #2962
[9] Ibid., #572
[10] Ibid., #2588
[11] Ibid., #2133
[12] Ibid., 547
[13] Ibid., #4382
[14] Ibid., #3833
[15] Ibid., #2316
[16] Ibid., #3823
[17] Ibid., #4561
[18] Ibid., #129
[19] Ibid., #746
[20] Ibid., #2888
[21] Ibid., #1849
[22] Ibid., #4189
[23] Ibid., #3751
[24] Ibid., #4024
[25] Ibid., #225
[26] Ibid., #2382
[27] Ibid., #1343
[28] Ibid., #4228
[29] Ibid., #5265
[30] Ibid., #2091
[31] Ibid., #2375
[32] Ibid., #4102
[33] Ibid., #4448
[34] Ibid., #956
[35] Ibid., #4030
[36] Ibid., #4992
[37] Ibid., #3162
[38] Ibid., #4151
[39] Ibid., #4336
[40] Ibid., #69
[41] Ibid., #5190
[42] Ibid., #3870
[43] Ibid., #861

About the Author

DR. LEE ANN B. MARINO, PH.D., D.MIN., D.D.

Dr. Lee Ann B. Marino, Ph.D., D.Min., D.D. (she/her) is "everyone's favorite theologian" leading Gen X, Millennials, and Gen Z with expertise in leadership training, queer and feminist theology, general religion, and apostolic theology. She has served in ministry since 1998 and was ordained as a pastor in 2002 and an apostle in 2010. She founded what is now Sanctuary Apostolic Fellowship Empowerment (SAFE) Ministries in 2004. Under her ministry heading Dr. Marino is founder and Overseer of Sanctuary International Fellowship Tabernacle (SIFT) (the original home of National Coming Out Sunday) and The Sanctuary Network, and Chancellor of Apostolic Covenant Theological Seminary (ACTS).

Affectionately nicknamed "the Spitfire," Dr. Marino has spent over two decades as an "apostle, preacher, and teacher" (2 Timothy 1:11), exercising her personal mandate to become "all things to all people" (1 Corinthians 9:22). Her embrace of spiritual issues (both technical and intimate) has found its home among both seekers and believers, those who desire spiritual answers to today's issues.

Dr. Marino has preached throughout the United States, Puerto Rico, and Europe in hundreds of religious services and experiences throughout the years. A history maker in her own right, she has spent over two decades in advocacy, education, and work for and within minority spiritual communities (including African American, Hispanic, and LGBTQ+). She has also served as the first woman on all-male synods, councils, and panels, as well as the first preacher or speaker welcomed of a different race, sexual orientation, or identity among diverse communities. Today, Dr. Marino's work extends to over 150 countries as she hosts the popular *Kingdom Now* podcast, which is in the top 20 percentile of all podcasts worldwide. She is also the author of over 35 books and the popular Patheos column, *Leadership on Fire*. To date, she has had five bestselling titles within their subject matter: *Understanding Demonology, Spiritual Warfare, Healing, and Deliverance: A Manual for the Christian Minister*; *Ministry School Boot Camp: Training for Helps Ministries, Appointments, and Beyond*; *Discovering Intimacy: A Journey Through the Song of Solomon*; *Fruit of the Vine: Study and Commentary on the Fruit of the Spirit*; and *Ministering to LGBTQ+ (and Those Who Love Them): A Primer for Queer Theology* (and its accompanying workbook).

As a public icon and social media influencer, Dr. Marino advocates healthy body image (curvy/full-figured), representation as a demisexual/aromantic, and albinism awareness as a model. Known to those she works with, she is a spiritual mom, teacher, leader, professor, confidant, and friend. She continues to transform, receiving new teaching, revelation, and insight in this thing we call "ministry." Through years of spiritual growth and maturity, Dr. Marino stands as herself, here to present what God has given to her for any who have an ear to hear.

For more information, visit her website at kingdompowernow.org.

www.ingramcontent.com/pod-product-compliance
Lightning Source LLC
LaVergne TN
LVHW051121080426
835510LV00018B/2157

9781940197364